Tragedy strikes on a wedding day ... ...e strength to go on living. A father bears his grief, stoically. A baby sister pours her sorrow into letters to her fallen brother. Through the pages of Susan's letters to Mark, another story emerges. A brief history of how a strategically crucial part of the Vietnam war was fought in a forbidding place by small units of outnumbered, outgunned Special Forces troops, supported by pilots who flew into the teeth of fire to bring them out alive. It is also a story of men whose loyalty to each other led them to perform acts of impossible bravery. Men who truly died for each other.

This must have been a painful book to write, but I'm sure that it will bring comfort somewhere to someone Susan doesn't know.

-Heywood Gould, author/screenwriter COCKTAIL

Susan Jimison has beautifully stitched her memories into a journey of discovery that celebrates the men who served with her brother and the ideals that carried them through a troubled time. *Dear Mark* will make you cry, but for a very worthy reason: it brings to life a good brother, a good man, and other good men who served with him, and who helped his youngest sister tell us not how he died, but how he lived.

-Deborah Smith, New York Times bestselling author A PLACE CALLED HOME

In our youth we don't imagine losing our siblings, but when loss occurs, the certainty is that life goes on. In her candid, skillfully crafted compilation of letters to her brother, Mark, who was killed in Vietnam combat, Susan shares with the reader the dimension in which she continues life with Mark. As she discovers how he lived, her profound love for him shines like a light throughout. In *Dear Mark* is the clear message that we should always remember the selfless dedication of those, who, like Mark, gave their all in the name of duty and their love of humanity. This book really has no ending, for Susan has much to share with her brother about life ahead. This is an inspiring page-turner for all ages, from all walks of life.

-Wayne Mutza, Author HELICOPTER GUNSHIPS

Gold Star Family member losses have been minimized and forgotten. This moving book brings them home to us as well as documenting a sister's search for information on her brother, and the wonderful Vietnam helicopter pilots who helped her and took her into their hearts.

-Patience Mason, author RECOVERING FROM THE WAR: A GUIDE FOR ALL VETERANS, FAMILY MEMBERS, FRIENDS AND THERAPISTS.

DEAR MARK

DEAR MARK

Susan Clotfelter Jimison

Deeds Publishing | Atlanta, Georgia

Published by Deeds Publishing
Marietta, GA
www.deedspublishing.com

Printed in The United States of America

Library of Congress Cataloging-in-Publications Data is available upon request.

ISBN 978-1-941165-09-6

Books are available in quantity for promotional or premium use. For information, write Deeds Publishing, PO Box 682212, Marietta, GA 30068 or info@deedspublishing.com.

First Edition, 2014

10 9 8 7 6 5 4 3 2 1

Dear Mark is dedicated
to the families of the fallen engraved on The Wall.

No event in American history is more misunderstood than the Vietnam War. It was misreported then and is misremembered now.

—**Richard M. Nixon**

FOREWORD

IN 1969 I WAS A young Special Forces sergeant, leading an eight-man recon team on top secret missions along the Ho Chi Minh Trail in southern Laos and northeastern Cambodia. Often misrepresented as mere coolies pushing bicycle-borne supplies on dirt paths, the Trail actually was a 2500-mile network of roads, over which 10,000 North Vietnamese trucks carried thousands of tons of supplies and tens-of-thousands of soldiers to the battlefields of South Vietnam.

Our unit, the Studies and Observations Group (SOG), was organized to covertly reconnoiter and disrupt that effort, doing our best to make the enemy pay a price for each mile traveled, for each weapon he delivered to South Vietnam. We did our best to achieve that.

However, the North Vietnamese were doing their best to stop us. To call the Trail heavily defended is an understatement: More than 50,000 enemy troops occupied and secured that road network, under a protective umbrella of nearly 10,000 anti-aircraft guns. To penetrate it and return—alive—was only due to our outstanding helicopter crews, especially our Cobra gunships from the 361st Aviation Company, Escort, nicknamed, The Pink Panthers. Each pilot wore a colorful patch depicting that cartoon character in a top hat, a cigar propped in its mouth and tossing rockets earthward.

The Pink Panthers always came through—ALWAYS. Many times, amid desperate gunfights with enemy forces, those Cobras would come in so low that I could see their faces through the Cobra's canopy, oblivious to ground fire. Some situations were so seemingly hopeless, that just the sound of their approaching rotor blades restored confidence. These crews saved our lives so often that (and this is the truth) it became ordinary.

One of those gutsy pilots was 21-year-old Warrant Officer Mark Clotfelter. I cannot say that I knew Mark in the one-to-one sense, but I can say with certainty that I met him at our launch sites before insertion or after yet another harrowing extraction from some dangerous situation. I hardly knew him, yet he repeatedly saved my life, along with that of many of my comrades and their recon teams, while risking his own. I cannot minimize that danger—twice he was shot down over Laos, and each time plucked from danger by our Huey helicopters.

By mid-1969, a Special Forces camp only ten miles north of our launch site at Dak To, had been encircled by two enemy regiments—some 5,000 soldiers—for five months. This camp, Ben Het, was so completely cut off and surrounded by anti-aircraft guns that supplies had to be delivered by cargo planes dropping parachute bundles. I know that situation well because I was there, both at Dak To, and later on a mission in the hills overlooking Ben Het.

On 16 June, several Cobra gunships, including Mark's, escorted a South Vietnamese convoy attempting to break through the encirclement and carry desperately needed supplies from Dak To to Ben Het. Mark and his fellow crewman, Warrant Officer Michael Mahowold, were overhead, providing supporting fire, when an awful ambush laid waste that convoy.

As one account reports:

In mid-June the South Vietnamese succeeded in getting a road convoy into Ben Het. But for more than a week after that, NVA ambushes and mines prevented further success. ARVN officers admitted to losing 27 vehicles. Hanoi radio broadcasts claimed some 183 had been destroyed. The road between Dak To and Ben

Het was littered with the carcasses of burnt-out trucks and other vehicles.

For the third time, Mark was shot down, and this time he, and fellow crewman Mahowold, paid the ultimate price. At the time of Mark's loss, his younger sister, Susan, was about to enter high school. Clearly, she admired her big brother, and this book is a product of that love. In it, she shares her thoughts and recollections with him. In it, she writes letters to him, "Just like I wrote when he was stationed in Texas, Alabama and Vietnam." This collection of letters is her shrine to him, her sharing of thoughts and memories.

But there are other shrines to Mark. These are the many grandkids today who know their grandfathers because Mark and the Pink Panthers were there, with the courage and flying skill to preserve their lives when five decades ago all seemed to be lost.

As I write these words, two grandsons are saying good night to my wife who is tucking them in. In your next letter, Susan, please thank Mark for me.

JOHN L. PLASTER
Command & Control Central,
MACV-SOG, 1968-1971

PROLOGUE

NOVEMBER 10, 2012

THE GRASS IS DAMP WITH dew and I'm fifth in line for the podium. Everyone in line is holding their list of thirty names they have the honor to read. It's the thirtieth anniversary of the dedication of The Vietnam Veterans Memorial in Washington, D.C. My list includes my brother Mark's name, as well as the co-pilot who died with him on June 16, 1969.

Cold—it's only in the upper 30s. I'm warm in my green flight jacket though—complete with Mark's original unit patch, name tag, and the U.S. Army tag he wore in Vietnam. I'm also wearing the miniature silver Army aviator wings Mark gave our Mother in 1968.

My sister Linda and I have already stopped by Mark's panel to leave a picture of Mark and the words to a song I leave every time I'm here. Paula Jones, the songwriter and singer, gave me permission to use her song many years ago. *"Brother of mine, I miss you so."* Leaving a picture is important to me. I think it makes it more real when you can put a face to the name— especially for the bus loads of school kids that will visit this holiday weekend.

It's early in the morning, quiet and serene. The only sound I am aware of is the voice of an older man standing at the podium. Wearing a red jacket with the Marine Corps emblem on the back, he speaks slowly into a microphone, reading his list of names. The speakers are facing about four dozen empty chairs that face the stage. They will be filled tomorrow for the Veteran's Day ceremony, and many more chairs will be added. It will be standing room only. But now, it's early, and not too many people have ventured in to D.C.—yet.

An occasional plane flies beyond the Lincoln Memorial and is loud enough to partially drown out the reader.

This is the third time I've had the honor to participate in the reading of over 58,200 names during the four days prior to the Veteran's Day ceremony. It's only the fourth time the names have all been read aloud here. From 6 AM to 11 PM every day—a family member, a friend, or a volunteer will read name after name, in the order they were taken from us, until every name on the Wall is read.

I used to know how many times I had visited D.C. but I quit counting years ago. Each trip is special, meaningful. So I go as often I can. It's the only place I feel Mark's presence—his burial ground, so-to-speak. Sacred ground.

Mark's ashes were scattered over the Atlantic Ocean in 1969. There was no headstone, no grave-side service. So for me, Panel 22 West, line 57—the side that catches the reflection of the Washington Monument—is where I feel Mark was laid to rest. This is where I come to talk to him. This is where he has remained forever young. And he, from the other side of his panel, has seen me grow from twenty-eight, the age I was when the Wall was dedicated, to fifty-eight, the age I am now. He knows Daddy's gone and Mother is too fragile to come here anymore because I've told him. He's seen my children grow, too, because of the numerous times I've brought them here. And now they bring their own children.

The in-between times—when I have lived too far away to visit—I wrote Mark letters about the ups and downs in my life. Just like I wrote him when he was stationed in Texas, Alabama, and Vietnam. I used to close my letters with "*be careful*" and he always closed his with "*write when you can.*" And so I do.

When I signed in this morning and picked up my reader's packet in the tent across the street, I looked through the bag to see what was in it. My assigned list of names, the time to be standing in line, and the exact time I would read. There was added instruction: *only read the names*—no additional words. There are two brochures, a lanyard commemorating the anniversary, a window cling, and a poster of The Wall. The red, white and blue of eleven American flags across the base of the panels in the poster is striking. I like the sun's reflection, with a silhouette of a tree in the center. The words under it …*I think of you often…I think about how different the family would have been…I love you and I miss you. You will always be in my heart.*

This poster says exactly what is in my heart. It's a keeper—I'll frame it when I get home.

When it's my turn to read, the volunteer at the top of the steps asks me to "read slowly because we are ahead of schedule and be careful of the ice when you head down the exit ramp." It *is* November, but ice hadn't entered my mind this morning so I walked carefully across the stage. When I reach the podium and look up from my list of names I see Linda with the camera ready to catch a memorable moment in my life. Slowly I begin:

Edward Voyt

Donald Lee Wickline Jr.

Mitchell Blaine Wysel

Gary Dean Bender

Rondal Lee Burns

And my brother, Mark Dennis Clotfelter…

SEPTEMBER 11, 1996

Dear Mark,

My heart is filled with so much sadness. So much hurt. It's the saddest, worst day since the day you died.

Daddy didn't wake up this morning.

I went to work at 5:30 today, and around 7:30 my supervisor came in and said Elsie had called to tell me Daddy had died in his sleep. Died? Oh my God, I wish I was better prepared for this. I didn't know what to do except grab my purse and leave work in a blur of tears.

By the time I reached my car I knew there were phone calls to make. Instead of telephoning our sister Nida, I went to the bus barn and waited for her to get in from her morning school bus run. She is as stunned as I. We just can't stop crying.

Since I moved to Poulsbo, Washington, a year ago, it seems Daddy has not been well. Not sick, really. Just not well. I went with him to the doctor many times, though, in the last year. I'm not sure how long he has lived with congestive heart failure. Maybe twenty years. But he didn't really seem sick. He almost made it to seventy-seven.

Nida and I are just numb. But next we had to call sisters, Linda and Redina, and of course Mother needed to know. I really didn't know how Mother was going to take it so I called Mike at work first and he took care of breaking the news to Redina and then of course, because Mother lives with Redina, Redina told Mother. No one expected this—I guess that's why we are all so stunned.

Now what? I never imagined life without Daddy. Just like I never imagined life without you.

You know we never talked about you, Daddy and me. It's been twenty-seven years now and we not once ever talked about you. We all just kept it inside. Maybe we knew if we started talking about you, we may not stop crying. Just like we never talked about Daddy's military service during World War ll. I know he was a waist gunner/radio man on a B-24. Maybe you two talked about it before you went to Vietnam? I wish I knew. Growing up, I thought it odd that he never watched war movies. Not even the John Wayne ones. Everyone else in the house did. Remember? We loved those old movies.

So, I guess now we'll never know what it was like for Daddy flying those missions in the South Pacific. I was always curious—I wanted to know, but was too afraid to ask. Mother says he came home with battle fatigue. They call that PTSD now. She says that's why he was sent to North Africa in 1951, during the Korean War, to set up radio relay stations. He just couldn't bring himself to go back into another combat zone.

Maybe it isn't too late to find out about your time in Vietnam. The guys you were stationed with would all be in their fifties now. I think I'll drag out your old pictures soon and see if somehow I can identify someone. If I locate the pilots you flew with, maybe I can learn more about you as an Army aviator, rather than just my big brother.

It's too late now to ask Daddy anything, and for that I am deeply saddened. But it has opened my eyes to what I may be able to learn about you—before it's also too late.

Today we lost the foundation of our family. Our "Rock of Gibraltar." You could always lean on Daddy—he was always there for us. And he took care of things. Like when you died. He handled everything. Probably the hardest thing he ever did in his entire life. How do you bury your only son? The one who worked on cars side-by-side with you? The one who became a ham radio operator, like you? The one who followed in your footsteps by getting a pilot's license and then going off to war—like you? How do you handle that?

Daddy was a strong man, a hard-working man. Sometimes toiling at two jobs—without complaint—to provide for our family. There were times we were pretty poor—but never felt poor. We didn't always have as much as the neighbors, but we always had what we needed.

Mark, you know how Daddy lived by the Golden Rule: "Do unto others as you would have them do unto you." Daddy helped neighbors with repairs and installations and never expected anything in return. They came to rely on him. There wasn't much Daddy couldn't do—from TV repairs to wiring a house to laying cement blocks to painting airplanes. A couple of years ago, a guy driving home from work in a Honda broke down in front of Daddy's house. Daddy fixed the stranger's timing chain, including buying the parts he needed. And, in return, he never asked for a dime. Daddy could afford to do so, but I think he remembered when he couldn't—and maybe this stranger couldn't. Daddy had a sense for things like that.

I'm not sure what I believe happens when we die. Is Daddy there with you now? I hope so, but I miss him so much here—right now.

Love, Susie

P.S. I wish you were here, so we could all do this together.

There are many reasons why this very real war has not been communicated to the reader at home. I had to come here to find what some of them are. In all wars of our experience, we have been able to put pins in a map—to move them ahead or back as the armies advanced or retreated. This is no longer possible. The enemy is in front of us, behind us and often among us.

—John Steinbeck,
Steinbeck in Vietnam 1967

OCTOBER 1996

Dear Mark,

Call it naiveté or just plain ignorance. I thought because a Vietnamese had shot you down, I should hate the Vietnamese. I am embarrassed to admit this after all these years. But I found a newspaper article and Letter to the Editor Daddy had cut out and saved for years. It really opened my eyes.

The Letter to the Editor was written by a Vietnam veteran who wrote, "Today would be different and forever alter my long held back thoughts of the Vietnam War in which I served in 1969, some 20 years ago."

Just before Veteran's Day 1989, Ed Page was having lunch with his wife and daughter in Poulsbo, Washington. On the cashier's counter he had noticed two neatly-framed medals, with an American flag background. He knew the medals well, the Vietnam Service Medal and the Republic of Vietnam Campaign Medal. He had them both.

In the frame's corner, a hand printed note simply stated, "Viet-Vets, The Manager Wants to Thank-You."

When the manager came to his table, Ed said the traditional "Chao Ba." Chung Nguyen, the restaurant co-owner responded, "When were you there?" Ed told him 1969-1970 in Pleiku and An Khe in the Central Highlands. Without hesitation Chung extended his hand in a sincere handshake and said,

"Thank you for defending my former homeland, thank you for serving my new country and welcome home to you." Soon a complimentary dish of egg rolls came out of the kitchen. It was just another way for Chung to say thank you.

In the twenty years since Ed Page had returned from Vietnam, he had never heard that thank you from any other person.

Ed wrote the editor, "Here, not a week before Veteran's Day, 1989, a Vietnamese refugee, in one small sincere gesture has taught me the true lesson of Veteran's Day. I have rarely been caught off guard about my emotions in regard to my Vietnam service. I was speechless. I realized these refugees are people who know and understand the sacrifices made by Vietnam vets far better than anyone. I had hit my personal wall, and I came out better for it."

The short story written about the restaurant owners was prompted by Ed Page's Letter to the Editor in the North Kitsap Herald. The photo at the top of the article shows the two young men holding the small frame Ed wrote about. In the interview with Chung and his partner Ngau Luong, Chung said, "It was my idea" to frame the medals but his partner shares in the "warm gratitude towards U.S. servicemen who served in Vietnam."

Ngau served in the South Vietnamese Army prior to leaving his country in 1983. Chung had been too young to serve during the Vietnam War, but carries a huge burden —the loss of his brother, a captain in the South Vietnamese Army, killed in the war in 1974.

Chung and Ngau met in 1988 during Chinese New Year and later decided to open the Golden Lion, a Chinese restaurant.

"We can give a handshake and a little egg roll or something" Chung said. "It's just my appreciation. Nothing can be changed now. But the feelings are still there. We were brothers then and we are brothers now."

After reading these articles, I felt compelled to go down to the Golden Lion. It was only ten minutes away, why not? I didn't know what I wanted to say, but felt the words would come when I got there.

When I arrived I only saw women, so I asked the hostess if Chung was there. She nodded and turned to a younger woman and spoke in what sounded like Vietnamese or Chinese and said what I thought must have been "go get Chung."

I had the articles in my hand when a short Asian man came from the back. He came up to me with a smile on his face, I introduced myself. I told him I had found the articles in my father's things who had recently died. He looked down to see what I was holding. He told me he remembered them well, and that he still sees Ed Page from time to time. I was honest with him and said I was not sure why I came down to meet him except my brother, too, had been killed in the Vietnam War. His smile was now gone and he told me how sorry he was and how forever grateful he would be to my brother and to my family.

We sat down in a booth while he told me of the oppression and communism in South Vietnam. Some of his family remains there, too old, too poor, or too sick to leave. The war was hard on everyone.

Like Ed, it was an unusual experience for me to hear the words of gratitude from a Vietnamese. I realized all the years I loathed the Vietnamese were unfounded. I learned the North Vietnamese were the enemy and the South Vietnamese were the ones you went over there to help. Seems simple now. But I didn't get it back then.

I still see Chung from time to time. His face lights up the moment our eyes meet. He has since opened a Pho soup and teriyaki restaurant. His success is obvious by the lack of seating or the wait to get our take-out food.

Sometimes I look around the restaurant and know that Chung and I share a past not many know about. There is no need to talk about the past anymore with Chung. It is our deep loss in our unspoken connection that we remember the moment our eyes meet.

You would like Chung!
Love, Susie

Above all, Vietnam was a war that asked everything of a few, and nothing of most in America.

—Myra MacPherson , Author of
*Long Time Passing: Vietnam and the
Haunted Generation*

APRIL 1997

Dear Mark,

You are not going to believe what has happened! I hardly know where to begin....

First off, I finally dragged out your pictures from Vietnam. It has been seven months since Daddy died and I was ready to look for someone who might remember you from Flight School or Vietnam.

I knew you were with the 361st Aviation Company, Escort. That was included on most of the documents from the Army, plus I still have the unit patch you wore in Vietnam. You know, the patch with protective plastic sewn around it and a button hole at the top? Complete with a Pink Panther smoking a cigar and holding what looks like rockets to me.

Initially, with a magnifying glass, I tried to identify the men in your old pictures. I could read a few of their last names on the front of their uniforms. Nida then looked up those names on the Internet and brought me a list of possible matches. She has been a great sister to help me out with this! I began mailing letters from the list, with hopes that I would find the right one. I enclosed a self-addressed stamped envelope with each so I would hear back whether or not they had been in Vietnam with you.

Without waiting on responses to those letters, I began posting on Vietnam Veterans online message boards, on a hand-me-down computer, that I was looking for someone who might remember you. I first heard from Art Cline, a kind, white-bearded man, who flew Cobras in Vietnam. He spread the word on an online list server. That's how Jack Taber, your classmate at Fort Rucker, contacted me. He told me you two were in Flight Class 68-9. We chatted about Vietnam and The Wall in D.C., and then Jack said, "In the Army we never leave a man behind, and that means family, too."

He vowed to help me find someone who remembered you from Vietnam.

I mailed him one of your snapshots to see if he could identify any of those men. The moment he opened the envelope he called me to say he recognized Bob Whitford, and that he knew how to get ahold of him!

My head was spinning with all this new information. And emotionally—it was moving so fast, after so long. It was getting harder to hold it together. After all it has been twenty-eight years since you died.

I received an e-mail right away from Bob Whitford. I found out he was not only a Pink Panther, he was also at Flight School with you and flew to Vietnam with you. He e-mailed he would be calling that evening!

Quickly, I let Jack know that Bob and I had connected. He e-mailed me back saying he knew Bob would be of help, that he was and still is a class act! He also told me that you are with us in spirit and they were happy to make my quest a reality. Oh—and that he would tip the next ale to you!

It was hard to pull myself away from the computer, but I had to pick up Scotty from school. You wouldn't believe how much he has grown! Nine years have just flown by. You would never know he's my son. Brown hair, brown eyes, and he tans beautifully. You and I always fried in the hot Florida sun!

By the time I returned, there was a message from Gary Higgins on my answering machine. His message was short, explaining who he was and that he would call back soon. I knew from all the pictures you had taken of Gary that you two must have been pretty close. I replayed the message several times. I didn't know what I wanted to say, but I couldn't wait to talk to both Bob and Gary.

I called Linda, Redina, and Nida to tell them the news.

As the phone calls began to come from the Pink Panthers, I tried to gather my thoughts and certainly didn't want to sound like your fourteen-year old little sister! I'm forty-three now and I needed to sound like it!

After the first two phone calls I realized what I wanted to know, and knew without a doubt what I didn't want to know.

Since 1969, I felt like there was enough documentation from the military that I already knew how you died. What I really wanted to know was how you lived. I wanted to know what you did when you were working. I wanted to know what you did when you weren't. I wanted to know what you did for fun.

I wanted to know how you lived the last nine months of your life.

After many e-mails from as far away as South Africa and phone calls as close as Seattle, I was invited to the Vietnam Helicopter Pilots Association reunion in Orlando, in just three months.

The Pink Panthers sent me a plane ticket for the reunion, plus arranged for my hotel room. I couldn't wait to go!

Love, Susie

P.S. It is hard to believe this is really happening!

War is what brought us together when we were young and changed us from strangers into a band of brothers. With the exception of the bond between a mother and her child, the brotherhood of those who fought together in battle may be the deepest bond that human beings ever form.

—Howard T. Prince II,
Brigadier General, USA, Retired

JUNE 1997

Dear Mark,

You might be surprised to know your old black flight bag is still around! After Daddy died I ended up with it. Well, it wasn't quite that simple. After the *North Kitsap Herald* published a story "Keeping a Brother's Memory Alive" and the fact that I was going to Orlando to meet your Army buddies, Daddy's widow, Elsie, called and said if I wanted your old bag I could come get it. She hasn't been real happy with me since I don't go over there much these days. We girls didn't appreciate how she sold Daddy's things off to the highest bidder, and then sold the rest of Daddy's stuff in a yard sale. We were in the grieving mode—Elsie was in the selling mode! I don't stew about it these days like I did back then. I didn't hesitate to go when I got the call though—thinking Elsie might change her mind. Driving over, I remember thinking how surprised I was that the bag had not been included in the yard sale! I discovered there wasn't a whole lot in it, but what was in it were old things that must have meant something to Daddy.

There was an old Father's Day card from you and a yellowed newspaper article about a high school classmate of yours, also killed in Vietnam. The classmate was also in the flying program you were in at Miami Dade Junior College. Richard Mc-

Nabb was killed July 21, 1969. Ten days earlier he had sent home a poem someone in his unit had written with hopes his young wife, Marilyn, could get it published in the local paper. It was published directly under the article about Richard dying in Vietnam. I am sure Daddy didn't know him but he must have thought you had because the article had your name in it also. The poem is so poignant I think it is worth passing on:

> *What a Soldier Gives*
> *Take a man and put him alone,*
> *Put him thirteen thousand miles from home.*
> *Drain his heart of all but blood,*
> *Then make him live in slime and mud.*
> *That's the life we have to live,*
> *And why my soul to God I give?*
> *You peace boys talk from an easy chair,*
> *But you don't know what it's like out there.*
> *You take your pills and have your fun,*
> *And then you refuse to lift a gun.*
> *I'll hate you till the day I die,*
> *Because you made me hear my buddies cry.*
> *I saw an arm, a bloody shred,*
> *And I heard them say 'this one is dead.'*
> *It's quite a price you had to pay*
> *So you could see another day.*
> *He bought your life by giving his,*
> *But who gives a damn what a soldier gives?*

There were also two letters written to Mother and Daddy, both dated March 1970 in response to letters written by Daddy. One from Brigadier General James Hughes who had been contacted by Congressman Claude Pepper:

A tragic death such as Mr. and Mrs. Clotfelter's son in the service to his country is always a source of deep personal sadness to the President. Additionally, the President knows how much it means to those who lost loved ones in Vietnam and their desire to have the Commander-in-Chief make the presentation. Although the President would like to personally present the awards earned by our deceased heroic servicemen to their families, this is not physically possible. Because of the number of awards earned in Vietnam, the President has limited his participation to the Nation's highest award, the Medal of Honor.

Didn't he mean because of the enormous number of deaths in Vietnam?

In all other cases, it is necessary for the President as Commander-in-Chief of the Armed Forces to be represented by other officials ...

The other letter was from Congressman Pepper whom Daddy had contacted to be the liaison between them and the White House. Daddy wanted President Nixon to present your medals to them. His condolences were extended and he shared regrets that the President could not do the presentation. He also said the recipients of the Medal of Honor would be the only presentation the President would personally do.

Their grief was private but they were so very proud of you and wanted it recognized. I'm not sure who organized it but eventually the ROTC at the University of Miami did the presentation. We, as a family, attended on the college football field. I know Mother and Daddy were proud to accept the medals and did so graciously. I didn't understand the significance of them at the time. Throughout the presentation I think I was on auto-pilot. Still sad, still missing you, and trying to look appreciative for those people, spending their afternoon in South Florida's blazing hot sun—in full uniform. I know I had to have been much cooler in my short lavender dress.

Also in your flight bag was the article The Miami Herald did of the presentation, complete with a photo of Mother and Daddy looking down at your medals, framed to display on a wall. Odd, I don't remember them on a wall in the house in

Hialeah but we only lived in that house until I graduated in 1972. Maybe they weren't hung up in the early years.

In Poulsbo, Washington, the medals were placed side-by-side with Daddy's own medals in the house he built. I don't know why, but after Daddy died, Elsie kept them, even though she never knew you. Several months later, with my insistence, she finally let me take them to Mother, along with the flag that draped your coffin.

Mother hung your medals on her picture wall and has your flag now. I still have the things from your flight bag. It's hard to know what to do with stuff like this. I seem to just keep holding on to every little piece connected to you. Not sure if it keeps you closer to me or keeps me from letting you go.

Your little sister,
Susie

I sincerely regret the sorrow that my telegram and this letter have carried into your home. It is my earnest hope that your son's fine record of service will be a source of comfort to you in the days to come. My deepest sympathy is extended to you in your bereavement.
—**Kenneth G. Wickham, Major General**

JULY 5, 1997

Dear Mark,

Would you believe Linda and Dennis recently celebrated their thirty-fifth wedding anniversary? I ran across a family picture from their wedding. There you were, about fifteen, wearing a white dinner jacket. Maybe you were the best man or something. I can't remember because I was only seven. Sure was a long time ago! Anyway, Linda and Dennis decided to drive down from Atlanta to join me for what turned out to be an emotion-packed weekend in Orlando with your Army unit, the 361st.

I arrived in Florida wearing Washington State weather clothes, not Florida clothes. I had forgotten how hot it could get! I had not been back to Florida since I left in 1986. I took the airport shuttle to the Marriott and knew immediately the four other people on the shuttle were going to the same reunion. The men wore Vietnam Helicopter Pilots Association T-shirts.

When I entered the lobby of the Marriott, one of the first things I saw was someone in the lobby wearing a Pink Panther costume, so I introduced myself. It was Jack Jordan's wife, Bettie Lou. She was quick to take me to some of the guys that were in the lobby. One was Bob Whitford and another was Jack Taber! Then I met Jack Jordan and Rick Huff. I was pretty nervous at first, but everyone was so nice!

I met so many people, all at once, that if they hadn't been wearing name tags I would never have remembered any names. I, too, was given a name tag for the reunion. It had my name and sister of ... then your name. Funny, that started to make me feel closer to you already. I had never had such a visual connection of you and me.

I ran up to change clothes, leave my bags in the room, and hurried back down to Bob.

We sat in the lobby, going through your pilot flight logs I brought with me, and Bob explained the notations in them. There were Vietnamese places mentioned like Pleiku and Danang. He told me they were pretend places for training in Texas, while you were at Fort Wolters. I liked your personal notations, *did well* or *did bad*. I suspect you were hard on yourself. I have been told you were a great helicopter pilot by those who knew it first-hand. While we were looking through your logbook, more people who had just checked in came over to talk to Bob, and he introduced me to them. I found myself imagining how you would look now, at their age. Would you still have all that hair, maybe still have your flat top haircut? Would you be thin, like I remember you? Maybe you would have gray hair...

Later we went to a hospitality suite that the Pink Panthers had upstairs. It was huge, a lot bigger than my spacious room. A kitchen, a bar, rooms at each end with beds, a large area with chairs and couches, two bathrooms. I overheard how they all split the cost and chip in for all the wine and beer. It is the hang out for all the Pink Panthers. Even guys from other units stop in. You would love it. Beer on tap and good company whenever you walk in.

Gary Higgins arrived while pictures were being taken late that afternoon in the Panther Suite. I didn't recognize him from your pictures; he is now turning gray. He arrived with his wife, Deborah, and he immediately joined the group for the photo—but before the picture was taken, before anything else happened, the world seemed to stop for two minutes as

Gary and I hugged. A hug I will never forget. It was a surreal moment. I have moved pictures of Gary around for thousands of miles, for twenty-seven years, knowing he and you had shared many moments—some good, some bad—and you and he shared the last several months of your life. Many times I have looked at his pictures, even talked to them, with hopes of someday learning more about you and what you did. And that day finally came. This is Gary Higgins!

The next day, Gary, Linda, and I sat down and talked about you. He still has a little red journal he kept while in Vietnam. In it were details—right down to the size of the holes on the aircraft when you two were hit by enemy fire. Then we watched a slide show of pictures from Vietnam that several guys had brought. Somehow I could look at your slides at home okay, but there—with your comrades and their pictures, pictures of you and the men sitting in this room—it hit me hard. Your loss is always real, but that day, it seemed like we were closer to 1969 when losing you was so emotional and raw.

Gary Higgins brought me a picture of you—a new picture of you. I never imagined I would have a new picture of you after all these years! I can't stop looking at it.

I even met Art Cline, the guy on the internet who responded to my very first post looking for someone who might have known you. He didn't know you but put me in touch with those who did. Because he responded that day, I began this incredible journey. For that I will be forever grateful to him.

Everyone had such nice things to say about you. And how they knew they could depend on you. Your first commanding officer, Major Rodgers, spoke very highly of you. He told me when you first got in-country you were very eager to learn the ropes and took everything very seriously, especially for a twenty-one -year old Warrant Officer. Commenting on you being a skillful pilot was followed up with telling me that you earned a Distinguished Flying Cross the month after you arrived in Vietnam. He also said you were well liked and fit in with the group. I think I may have been beaming when he was telling me all of this!

Rick Huff was so kind to sit down with me and tell me about missions, how good the maintenance guys were, and how great the camaraderie was. Further into our conversation he said the Panthers were always curious about the new guys—and thought you were unusual. While waiting for a mission the rest of the guys were napping or reading, but you might be crawling over a Cobra examining things and going "hmm" every few seconds. Then he told me about you tape-recording a lot of things and how you seemed much more intense than the rest of them. *Nonetheless, as we got to know him, he fit right in. We all liked and respected him, and he was a good pilot.* How nice it was to hear Rick tell me all this!

So, what a time I had in Orlando with your buddies from Vietnam. The most important thing I learned from the trip is they never forgot you! So many told me when they go to the Vietnam Veterans Memorial in D.C., they *always* touch your name. I can't begin to explain how that makes me feel. It warms my heart to know they never forgot you.

There was a banquet tonight in the hotel ballroom. I wore pink! Outside the ballroom, but inside the hotel, there were two helicopters on display. A Cobra and a small bubble type helicopter. I was told it was a LOH, pronounced Loach, and both were on a rolling platform. I was amazed they fit in the hotel!

Inside, more than two hundred tables that seat eight people, filled up. There were remarks, food, drinks, presentations, introductions, and a Missing Man Ceremony. Earlier, I had seen the table but didn't ask anyone about it. I didn't know what to expect when the Missing Man ceremony began, two Pink Panthers, one on my left, one on my right, reached for my hands. This is what I heard:

Your attention is directed to the small table located in a place of honor near the head of the banquet hall. It is a way of symbolizing the fact that some of our friends are missing from our midst.

They are unable to be with us this evening, so we remember them.

The table, set for one, is small—it symbolizes the frailty of all of us.

The tablecloth is white—symbolic of the purity of their intentions to respond to their country's call to arms.

The single rose displayed in a vase reminds us of the families and loved ones of our comrades who will not return.

The red ribbon, tied so prominently on the vase, is reminiscent of the red ribbon worn upon the lapel and breast of thousands who bear witness to the tragedy of POW's and MIA's and, with unyielding determination, demand a proper accounting for our missing.

A slice of lemon rests on the plate—symbolic of the tears of families and loved ones.

The glass is inverted—they cannot toast with us tonight.

The chair is forever empty—they are not here.

Tonight we take time to recall those who were our comrades-in-arms, we depended on them for aid and support.

Let us remember all of our missing crewmembers, and honor them as we stand for a moment of silence…

Tears fell because I still miss you. But also because, for decades, I felt the only people that ever thought about you was our family. These guys have not forgotten you and I don't think they ever will. They also acknowledged the tremendous sacrifice of the family, a new experience for me as well.

You would be proud of the way your Pink Panthers have welcomed me with open arms. They not only shared their past with me, to help me understand you as a warrior, but they also invited me into their future. Linda and I were given shirts with our names on them and the 361st patch, duplicated from the one you wore in Vietnam.

I have been invited to next year's reunion in Fort Worth, Texas. It includes a bus ride out to Fort Wolters, which is a closed base now, to see where you were first trained in a helicopter.

But what I really want to tell you is this: I wish you had been sitting at the banquet tonight, not me. Not Linda and Dennis. This is your reunion, not mine.

Rest in peace, dear brother. You are still missed.

Love, Susie

p.s. On the way to the airport tomorrow and probably the whole way back to Seattle, I want to tell you about meeting Julie. She is the first person I ever met who lost a brother in Vietnam.

THE COBRA

I positioned myself
In the backseat of the Cobra
Feeling a need to know
What it was like 28 years ago.

His spirit was with me
I felt peace and closeness
A better understanding
For Mark, 28 years ago.

I listened in awe as
You explained the procedures
From experience, with expertise
There was a passion I heard
For flying Cobras, 28 years ago.

My new big brothers
Took their time and cared
That I felt the need to know
Where Mark sat 28 years ago.

So many hours, day or night
Mark sat in the back seat
Like I was then
It felt good, it felt right
Like it was for Mark, 28 years ago.

Written for Bob Whitford and Jack Taber
Vietnam Helicopter Pilots Association Reunion
July 6, 1997
—Susan Clotfelter Jimison

I think it's safe to say the vast majority of us had our heads buried about Vietnam. That's one thing we have in common. It's like a pie shaped piece of my life—not my whole life by any means, but it is a piece that reaches to the very center, started out as a sliver and widens as it goes.

—Julie Kink, Gold Star sister

MY NEW SISTER JULIE

Dear Mark,

I'm flying home from Orlando now. So tired from not having enough sleep since landing in Florida. But I have settled into my window seat, which is perfect for writing and thinking, and to tell you all about a woman I met at the reunion. Her name is Julie Kink. Her brother David was killed in Vietnam the same summer we lost you.

Actually, I had been contacted by Julie Kink online when I first posted on the message boards in April, about my hope of finding someone that remembered you from Vietnam. We have communicated online since then, so it was great to finally meet her face to face.

Julie is the first person I've ever met who had lost her brother like I had. And like you, her brother was a helicopter pilot. We found other similarities, like we were both the youngest of the family, we both were eager to find out more about our brothers as adults, as warriors, and we had both experienced decades of silence, of no one talking about Vietnam. The only things we heard about our military were negative: baby killers, rapists, homeless, and drug addicts. The media perpetuated those lies for years.

Julie is six years younger than me, and sadly doesn't have as many memories of her brother as I do of you. She told me how wonderful she thought it was that I had so many memories, but at the same time, she thought it meant I lost so much more when you were killed. She added how it made her feel lucky to have only been eight. And that the times that I remember must play like a movie in my head! I never thought of it like that before.

I do feel fortunate to have so many good memories of you. Remember how the neighbors would rough-house and Daddy forbade you to ever put a hand on us girls? I told Julie about the times I would pause in front of the TV when you were watching it, and you always snapped, "You make a better door than a window!" And your snakes... I never liked them. Remember the motorcycle you bought with three-wheels and the big white box on the back like the Miami Beach cops had? And you rode me around the block while I sat on the box? Some things you never forget...the movie Julie mentioned is playing in full color!

During the reunion, Julie and I spent countless hours, into the wee hours of the morning, talking about our experience of losing our brother and how our families coped with that loss. Meeting another KIA sibling was equally important to both of us. We had kept our feelings inside for so long!

David Kink is buried in Wisconsin. Your ashes were scattered in The Atlantic Ocean is all I have known. I have always wished you had been buried somewhere. I guess a part of me feels I could have gone there to talk to you. On the anniversary of your death I used to take a carnation to the beach and toss it into the water. But I never felt like you were there, so I never talked to you at the beach. And eventually quit going on that annual trip. After Julie told me that people had vandalized David's grave during the war with spray paint a few times, I somehow felt fortunate our family didn't have to deal with the hatred. If you just kept quiet, no one knew.

I asked Julie what came to mind when she thought of David's personal belongings that came home from Vietnam. She said the smell and I agreed with her. The smell was musty but probably had less to do with Vietnam and more to do with being packed up and sitting somewhere in the heat and humidity for a long time.

She also told me, a few times, she has pictured David crawling from a burning helicopter, and a few months ago she learned that a white phosphorus grenade had detonated after his crash and burned him on the lower back and back of his legs as he was trying to make it out. She never knew that before and it made her so sad. But then those images passed quickly for her and every single time she thinks of David, he is standing tall beside her. She never pictures him burned, scared, feeling alone, worrying about death, or regretting his decision to go in the Army. He wouldn't want her to picture him that way. To her, he is whole, nineteen, filled with dreams, expectations, and love for what he is doing.

That is true for me, too. In my mind, I never picture you as anything except the handsome twenty-one-year-old who loved sports cars and flying. That is the way you will always look to me.

Julie and I are on the same path in life to learn as much as we can about you and David. On this path, we found each other, and we both know it is finally okay to talk about you and David, and Vietnam. Who knew that something so heart wrenching as losing you, there would emerge something so special, a new sister...

Love, Susie

…We're winged soldiers, we fly above the best,
Defenders of the land and the free,
From the sky we do or die and let the angels rest,
Winged soldiers are we.
Rotor blades are turning, diving for the fire,
Screaming in like eagles for the kill,
After our inferno, troopers must admire,
Eagles of the Army's escadrille.
We're winged soldiers, We fly above the best,
Defenders of the land and the free,
From the sky we do or die and let the angels rest,
Winged soldiers are we.
—**Army Aviation Warrant Officer Song**

WATERMELON PATCH

Dear Mark,

Funny how you all were grouped by last names throughout flight school. The guys I found from class 68-9—the ones that knew you best—all have last names beginning with a C. I still have a great letter received from your classmate, Doug Cooper, in '97.

Mark was a good friend. He was in our gang all the way through flight training at Ft. Wolters and Ft. Rucker. We were grouped together alphabetically, so we roomed next door to each other, flew together, went to the same classes, and most certainly got into the same trouble. Our section was known for being a tad "high spirited." A special chemistry.

I was there when we tossed Mark through the crossed helicopter rotor blades into the Holiday Inn swimming pool. Tradition after the first solo flight.

Some of us visited a farmer's field following engine failures, a too common experience. But there were two memorable farmer's field incidents one just can't forget!

One night we were flying cross-country during training in Texas. We usually flew a triangular-shaped route with small towns at the corners for check-points. Part of our flight encountered unexpected high headwinds on the return leg back to Demsey Army Heliport. The old OH-13 helicopters we were flying would only make about 70mph airspeed on a good day. The headwinds were 40 to 50 mph—not good when we only had 1.5 hours of fuel. Several guys had to land in remote areas because of low fuel. One ran out of gas in flight and had to auto-rotate into a farmer's field in total darkness. The autorotation is an emergency procedure we were all trained to do if the engine quit. A Huey from base flew in and picked up the two student pilots. The next morning two maintenance men from Wolters went to pick up the OH-13 with a trailer, only to be met by the farmer with a shotgun. He claimed the chopper was now his because it was on his property. The maintenance men left, but returned with the sheriff and a warrant, and finally the farmer allowed then to retrieve the government property.

The other incident was in Alabama at Ft. Rucker. We were flying the UH-1 during tactical training. During the previous couple of weeks we had flown low-level over a farmer's field of watermelons every day. Seems like every night someone would mention how the melons were getting big and ripe enough to pick. So one day, I believe it was Mark who came in to hover next to the patch while I was the "lookout" that circled above. I could be wrong about who it was—it's been so long. Then the co-pilot jumped out, ran over and "captured" two of the largest melons. After he stashed them in the back of the Huey, they flew back to the airfield. That evening we feasted with our WOC (Warrant Officer Candidate) friends. Imagine the farmer finding two of his prize melons missing and following the tracks into the middle of the field where they mysteriously end. He may have had some suspects in mind considering literally hundreds of the helicopter flights over his farm each day.

This is another time I wish Daddy was still with us. He would have enjoyed the stories about you—even the non-combat stuff. Especially something that happened in the state he grew up in. It sounded like something he would have done himself.

I love the stories Doug shared! See why I treasure each and every one of these Vietnam vets?

I've never seen a Huey hovering a farmer's field before, but I can almost picture it through Doug's memories.

The funny stuff sure helps with the sad stuff.

Love, Susie

There's teddy bears and high school rings and
old photographs that mamas bring
Of daddies with their young boy, playing ball.
There's combat boots, he used to wear,
When he was sent over there.
And there's 50,000 names, carved in the wall.

—50,000 Names by Jamie O'Hara

VETERANS DAY 1997

Dear Mark,

I just returned from Maryland after having a nice visit with
Mother, Redina, and her gang. We all went into D.C. yesterday
for the Veterans Day Ceremony. Mother wore her tan coat
with your miniature aviator wings pinned on it. She has always
had the helicopter charm hanging from one side—just as you
gave her in 1968. For years now she has worn it with a back
ribbon behind it. I have only guessed it must be an old custom
done when they have suffered a loss because I have never seen
anyone else do it. I never asked her why.

We parked at the last Metro Station in Maryland on the
Orange Line in New Carrolton. It's about a thirty minute ride
in on the train.

It turned out to be a beautiful, cool fall day. It's about a ten
or fifteen minute walk to the Memorial. Mother has always
done a lot of walking and at seventy-five had no trouble with
the walk from the Metro Station to the Wall.

Even though Mother has only seen the half scale traveling
replicas, when we had the Wall in sight, she walked a little
ahead of us and straight to your panel. On holidays like this
and Memorial Day, there are so many people gathered near
the Wall. Many things are left at the base of the panels. Teddy
Bears, medals, letters, and even half drunk beer cans left for
their comrade whose name is on the Wall. Nobody touches

them but most want to see what is left at the Wall. So people are squatting or kneeling, many are taking pictures, some just running their fingers over a name.

After we all caught up with her at your panel, and touched your name, we decided we needed to find a seat in the grassy area for the ceremony, so we wouldn't have to stand the entire time, but we ran into Jim Schueckler. He consistently volunteers here at the memorial every Veterans Day. He is one of the yellow hat volunteers that have pencils, plain paper with The Vietnam Veterans Memorial across the top, and ladders to assist in name rubbings. I first met Jim, also known as Polecat from his call sign in Vietnam, on the Vietnam Helicopter Flight Crew Network (VHFCN). This was the first time I had met him in person. He had printed papers with Army Aviator Wings to do a rubbing of Army pilots who were on the Wall. It was his own personal touch and tribute to the helicopter pilots who died in Vietnam. So I quickly did yours before we headed towards the chairs.

On the way to the seating area we ran into John Plummer, a Vietnam helicopter pilot and a minister now, whom I met in Orlando at the reunion this past July. I introduced Mother to him. John knew she was a Gold Star Mom. He hugged her. Mother seems to be more accepting of hugs the older she gets. We sure didn't grow up with hugs, did we?

We met up with my dear friend Julie Kink, and I introduced her to everyone. It sure was good to see her again. She was wearing her black Cav hat. I have learned the hat signifies belonging to a Cavalry unit. The hat seems to be the only reminder left of the days the Cavalry rode horses. Her brother was in the Cavalry unit called the 1st of the 9th. There's a pin on her hat that says "My Brother Served" with a tiny map of Vietnam. I have the same pin. We both bought them at the reunion in Orlando. Today I wore your original Pink Panther patch you had in Vietnam. I have it pinned well to my jacket, terribly afraid of losing it.

Getting to our seats we passed the front row filled with Gold Star Mother's. They wear all white. Their uniform, so to speak, includes a hat embroidered "Gold Star Mother," with gold piping on the edges. Our Mother would never think to join a group like that. A group she qualifies for, not by choice. Those women wear their hearts on their sleeve. Mother could never do that.

Emmy Lou Harris sang *America* and Jamie O'Hara sang *50,000 Names On The Wall*. Boy, that song got to everyone.

It was a nice ceremony. Most of the speeches were about remembering those whose names are on the Wall. They spoke of remembering them today...I remember you every day.

After the ceremony, Julie introduced me to her brother David's commanding officer from Vietnam, retired COL Robert Treadway. She was very lucky to have located him recently because she has learned so much about what happened the day David crashed. More than what was written in the Army documents. Julie and I hugged and went our separate ways. We won't see each other until next summer at the next reunion.

We walked back to the Metro. Onboard heading back to Maryland, Mother took those miniature wings off, and handed them to me. She said, "You'll wear these more than me now." I was stunned. We all were. No one said anything for a long time. I choked back any emotion. Stoic. Mother and Daddy's generation chose to not show any emotion and I thought that I should hold mine back, too. I held the wings in my hand the whole way home, and held in my emotions until I was alone in my bed for the night.

Laying in the dark that night, I thought of nothing else except the day you gave Mother those wings at Fort Rucker and today when she gave them to me. Bittersweet tears I guess.

We were all so happy the day you received your wings. Remember?

Mother knows I went to the reunion to meet your Army buddies in Orlando. Meeting John Plummer today may have opened her eyes to just how kind Vietnam vets have been to me. Whatever her reason for giving me the very wings you pinned on her the day you received your Aviator Wings, I will wear them proudly. I will wear them in honor of her and you.

The Vietnam Veterans Memorial is the only place where your name is etched. It is the place that says you were here on this earth. It's the place I feel closest to you. Almost like you are on the other side of that black granite, looking at me, looking at you. That reminds me of a song I love called *Brother of Mine*. In the song Paula Jones sings, "I'm all grown up now, you look the same." It is the song I leave at your panel every time I go.

I'm almost twice as old as you were when we lost you. I feel like you would have done so much more with your life than I have with mine. From here on out, I want to make sure your legacy is preserved. That our grandchildren know who you were and they pass it on to their children. I am writing everything down so when I am gone, everything I learned about you will be passed on.

You will be forever young!

Love, Susie

BROTHER OF MINE

Paula Marie Jones, Song Writer/Singer
paulamariejones.com

It was a cold fall day, to visit you
I didn't call ahead, no need to.
I come with pictures, flowers,
my mission and quest.
The book says your home is 15 west.
Brother of mine, I miss you so.

Reflections of your name;
I'm all grown up now, you look the same.
It's been years without you, do cuts always heal?
If I could only tell you how I feel.
Brother of mine, I miss you so.

I feel your touch, is that you on the other side?
I touch your name, is that you calling mine?
Sometimes it seems like you're just standing there;
looking at me, looking at you.

It was a cold fall day to visit you;
Darkness takes the sky, way too soon.
I'll be back one day, someday , I'll never forget!
How your hands touched mine, and spirits met.
Brother of mine, I miss you so.

I feel your touch, is that you on the other side?
I touch your name, is that you calling mine?
Will I ever know why you had to go?
Brother of mine, I miss you so.

> Death's errand boys do not come cloaked.
> They arrive in dress blues, wearing white gloves,
> their shoes spit-shined, their brass polished.
> —Jedwin Smith, Our Brother's Keeper

REMEMBERING JUNE 21, 1969

Dear Mark,

Everyone thinks of their father as being strong. I found out just how strong Daddy was on June 21, 1969. We all remember that day as the day Redina got married.

It was a Saturday morning and Nida and I were in the living room. There was a knock at the front door at 7:30. Daddy heard it as he came out of the kitchen and set his coffee cup down. He opened the door and let in two men wearing Army uniforms. Once inside they removed their hats but stood by the front door. Daddy didn't move back to let them in further. They had a short quiet discussion.

Daddy's back was to us so we could not see a reaction to what was being said. The two men departed and Nida and I were still standing near the kitchen. Noticing the Western Union telegram in his hand, Daddy turned to us and said, "We are not talking about this today."

"Missing" is what I overheard one of the soldiers say.

Missing…I thought, okay, you're missing: I was sure you were just lost in the jungle, but they would find you!

Daddy went directly into his bedroom where Mother was and closed the door. Nida and I just stood there. Almost like we were frozen. I was fourteen and Nida had just turned eighteen. We knew from the tone of Daddy's voice that we had better not say a word. It was a tone we had never heard before. We didn't say anything to each other or to anyone else.

The morning wedding at Hialeah Presbyterian Church went off as scheduled. It was a small wedding with family and friends, and the reception followed at our home. Seems like people were everywhere and there was no time to decipher what had happened that morning.

After the cake was cut and pictures were finished, the bride and groom left for their honeymoon on Miami Beach.

Watching the ceremony—where photographs were taken all day long—I kept remembering how you had introduced Mike to Redina in 1967, before he enlisted in the Air Force in 1968. Then you worked together at Aerodex by Miami International Airport. The day before the wedding Mike had flown in from Virginia where we was stationed at Andrews Air Force Base. Redina was now a military wife.

Once all the guests were finally gone Mother retreated to her bedroom. Linda and Dennis were still at our house when Daddy explained to all of us about that morning's telegram. Dated June 21, it said that on June 16 you were declared Missing In Action:

> " ....he was last seen as Commander of a military aircraft on a combat operation when the aircraft was fired upon by a hostile ground force, crashed, and burned. Search is in progress and you will be promptly advised when further information is received. In order to protect any information that might be used to your son's detriment, your cooperation is requested in making public only information concerning his name, rank, and service number....."

We were stunned. Daddy told us the facts. No speculating. No elaborating.

I silently reminded myself that you were only missing and would soon be found, ignoring the crashed and burned part. Daddy had experienced war, and without saying, knew this was only the preliminary to our worst fears. You were never coming home.

This telegram was the first of many to arrive at our house over the next several weeks. Mother and Daddy, the stoic generation, hid their grief from us. We never saw them cry.

I've never forgotten Daddy's strength that day to make that split-second decision to go through with Redina's wedding, knowing he probably had just lost his only son. He greeted people, walked his daughter down the aisle, and posed in countless wedding photos. But I know his heart must have been breaking.

That was happiest day of Redina's life but only because of Daddy's decision. Because of his strength.

I still remember it as the day Redina got married. But I will never forget it was also the day we lost you.

Love, Susie

> You could have a snake for thirty years and the second you leave his cage door cracked, he's gone...And they'll never come to you unless you're holding a mouse in your teeth"
>
> —Bill Haast

FLORIDA

Dear Mark,

Thinking back to growing up in South Florida, I could never understand why we took those who were visiting us to the Everglades! Daddy's mother, Mother's sister, Dennis's parents—anyone that came to visit—we hauled them out to the Everglades. Since when is swatting mosquitoes a good photo opportunity?

Then there was the beach, which was fun—to a point. But after all those sunburns, blisters and peeling...it forever altered my idea about the perfect vacation spot! You, Redina, me... blonde hair, blue eyes, fair skin—or should I say burnt skin?

Remember going to Miami International Airport just to watch the planes take off and land? We'd sit there for hours. Is that when your love for airplanes and flying began?

I can't remember the year, but I know after a trip to Bill Haast's Serpentarium with Daddy how you became a huge fan of Bill Haast, the Miami Snake Man. It was not a short trip down to Punte Gorda on U.S 1 where he built the Miami Serpentarium. Going there once was enough for me. But after you started driving, you went regularly. No use ever asking me if I wanted to go along for that ride—I still don't like snakes.

Bill Haast was brilliant. But his love for snakes and acquiring venom was too scary for me. His work—side-by-side with the University of Miami and all the hospitals, was world renowned. He was the go-to man for any snake bites—not only in the United States but anywhere in the world! His anti-venom saved many lives. I read about a woman that had a daughter going blind and the venom restored her vision. And a man with multiple sclerosis that believed venom injections were helping his debilitating condition. The Miami Snake Man was amazing!

I can see where you were drawn to him. You had a few snakes of your own.

Bill Haast is gone now, dying in 2011 at the age of one-hundred! The Miami Serpentarium is also closed, but his work lives on at the Miami Serpentarium Laboratories. All those snake bites, accidental or deliberate for scientific purposes, didn't appear to shorten his life.

Mr. Haast lived on the edge his whole life. And he liked it. Your life was somewhat like that while you were flying in Vietnam. The danger was always there and you liked it.

I wouldn't say you or Mr. Haast were thrill seekers, but what you were both doing was not only thrilling, but purposeful. Thrill seekers just do stuff for the emotional high. I think that's the big difference between thrill seekers and purposeful, thrilling lives. You and Mr. Haast made a difference!

Your little sister—still afraid of snakes,
Susie

Now come on mother's throughout the land,
Pack your boys off to Vietnam,
Come on fathers don't hesitate,
Send your sons off before it's too late,
Be the first one on your block,
To have your boy come home in a box.

And it's 1, 2, 3 what are we fightin' for?
Don't ask me, I don't give a damn,
the next stop is Vietnam,

And it's 5, 6, 7 open up your pearly gates.
Well there ain't no time to wonder why...
WHOO we're all gunna die.

—Country Joe and The Fish
War protest song

SUMMER 1971

Dear Mark,

In June 1971, Daddy and Mother sent me with a one-way ticket to stay with Mike and Redina for the entire summer. It had been two years since we lost you. Not sure if that had anything to do with getting rid of me for the summer. Maybe they just needed a break.

Mike was stationed at Offutt Air Force base in Omaha, Nebraska. Wow, is it hot there! The days were 100s plus, but the nights cooled down to the low 60s. Nothing like our summer weather in Florida. Remember? Hot in the morning, hot in the afternoon, hot in the evening. The heat never seemed to bother you though.

I was sixteen and had my driver's license, so when Redina and Mike were at work, I used their new orange Karmann Ghia to explore. Another contrast to Florida was the streets downtown. They were all so hilly that I had to learn quickly to use the gas, clutch and brake almost simultaneously! Luckily, I never backed down into anyone, but it was close at first. Learning to drive in Florida, where everything is flat, doesn't prepare you for hill driving.

Jim Morrison, lead singer for The Doors, died that summer on July 3 at the age of twenty-seven. I know his music wasn't your style. But I know you would recognize his music. Come on baby, light my fire. We've heard that a thousand times! Did you know he was from Melbourne, Florida?

On weekends we hung out, and sometimes went to the movies. On base it only cost a quarter. Redina and I saw *Wuthering Heights*. Emily Bronte wrote that book in the mid 1800s, and the movie was great! It was then I decided if I had a girl, I would name her Heather. And if I had a boy, I would name him Heath from the main character. Now you know where Heather got her name!

I ate real Chinese food for the first time that summer. It wasn't anything like the canned Chun King stuff Mother used to buy. We also went boating with some of Mike and Redina's military friends, and I water skied for the first time. Sounds kind of strange that someone from Florida learned to water ski in a land-locked state, but I did. I also learned no one should ski in a bikini. Too much force when you hit the water! I worried more about losing my bikini bottom than trying to stay upright on the skis!

You know how we never went to camp, right? Who could afford it with five kids? I had never been away from home for more than a week . So I corresponded with my girlfriends. And after a month or so, I started calling Mother and Daddy to ask when I could come home. Daddy didn't get his vacation until August and he kept saying no. I had to stay until he had enough time off to fly his Cessna 172 to get me. The four-seat airplane was not new, but new to us. Daddy worked hard to scrape the money together to buy it. I know all the while he thought about buying it, and while he worked on it getting it ready for the trip, he wished you had been there, too. It was just the kind of thing you two liked to do together. We had the perfect place to keep the airplane. Even though Daddy was still an electrician during the day, he started a business painting airplanes at Opa Locka airport at night and on the weekends. He even hired my friend Jeff Shaw to work for him.

While Mike and Redina worked on July 10, by pure happenstance I ended up driving into an anti-war protest at Memorial Park. Police used bull horns to talk to college students from the nearby university. The students were shouting back. I had never seen anything like it before, except on the six o'clock news. The Kent State National Guard shooting of four college students was still fresh in my mind. It was the previous year but they re-played it on television a hundred times. The chaos that erupted at Kent State University came on the heels of an announcement by President Nixon that the war was spreading into Cambodia. Years later, I found out you had been secretly flying across the border from Vietnam into Cambodia long before Nixon announced it. I guess the cat was out of the bag, and the students felt like widening the war into another country was making their draft more likely.

I saw police in riot gear, students with anti-war signs, squad car lights, and a bonfire. Through the flames, though, I could see that bonfire was actually a car. My window was down and I could hear someone beating on a drum, shouting, and I could smell something awful. Looking at the students I realized I kind of looked liked them. Long straight hair parted in the middle, I wore a peasant top and low-waist bell bottoms that dragged the ground.

But that was on the outside—on the inside I was very different. I was scared and angry, and I wanted to get out of there fast. I felt like all of it was directed at the soldiers fighting the war—like you—and I didn't want any part of it.

As I tried to drive away, people were walking directly in front of me trying to get to all the action that I was trying to get away from. I wanted to drive faster, but couldn't. When I finally got a safe distance away, I pulled over. Only then did I realize I was shaking, and tried to make sense of what looked like a senseless situation. I was relieved nothing happened to Redina's car. I didn't know how I would have explained that.

That night on the six o'clock news, there it was. The protest. Thankfully, I didn't see me or the orange Karmann Ghia! I didn't say anything to Redina about being there accidentally.

Finally, Daddy and Mother made the trip in August to bring me home. The Cessna 172, as you know, is not much faster than a car, so it took us several days to get home. Daddy didn't care. He was happy just to be flying, racking up air time!

I sure had a lot of new experiences that summer in Nebraska. Mostly good. Something that stayed with me forever—I saw many signs and shirts with Peace signs on them that day in Memorial Park. To me it represented the chaotic riots—anti-war. I also felt like it was anti-soldier. Because of that, I've never worn a Peace sign, drew one, or bought anything with a Peace sign on it because of the rioters. Never.

Ironically, today there is a war memorial in that same park honoring the very ones I felt those rioters despised.

Did you ever see the anti-war stuff before you went to Vietnam? Maybe you only saw it on television like I had before I went to Omaha? Somehow seeing it like that, in a box in the living room, isn't quite as real as hearing the crowd, smelling burning rubber and feeling your heart pound in your chest.

I think you may have been too busy training in 1968 to defend and protect our freedoms that gave the rioters the right to free speech to pay much attention to this stuff.

None of this matter's anymore. But because of that summer—that riot—I will never buy anything with a so-called "peace sign" on it.

Love, Susie

We gotta get outta this place
If it's the last thing we ever do…
—Eric Burden and the Animals

JULY 1998

Dear Mark,

I just returned from the Vietnam Helicopter Pilots reunion. This year it was held in Fort Worth, Texas. It was my second reunion, and this time I had my wits about me. Last year, my first time meeting the Pink Panthers seems more like a dream. Meeting so many people, while on an emotional roller coaster for days, keeps that a blur.

Julie and I shared a room at night, but went our separate ways during the day. Her brother David was in the 1st Squadron, 9th Cavalry Regiment, so her daytime was spent with CAV guys and mine was spent with your guys, the Pink Panthers. Sometimes we would meet up accidentally in an elevator or at a planned meeting for a quick beer or coffee. She was the only one in Texas at that moment—maybe even the world—that truly understood what being there with your unit felt like. We agreed it made us both feel closer to you and David even though you both have been gone twenty-nine years.

Several bus-loads from the reunion hotel went to Bell Helicopter headquarters for a tour and a demonstration on the airfield. The two helicopters I remember most were, of course, the Cobra and the V-22 Osprey with its tilted rotor. They were all really loud and seemed to be easily maneuverable. The crowd cheered! I couldn't help but think how you would have enjoyed it.

The next day we went to Fort Wolters, now a closed Army base. I saw the barracks and the place where the Warrant Officer dances were held on the weekends. While there, I was approached by Gary Thewlis, a Black Cat with the 213th Assault Support Helicopter Company, who asked if I would have an interest in working on a committee to help others, like Julie and me, to assist in locating someone who may have known their lost loved one who had died in Vietnam. I told him it would be my honor.

Knowing how I felt when I found your unit, I knew my heart and soul were in the right place to help others. He explained it was a labor of love, and the requests and assignments would all be online. So now I am on the Vietnam Helicopter Flight Crew Network Family Contacts Committee. I hope I am as successful with helping others as I was with locating your guys.

After we returned to the reunion hotel in Fort Worth, Tom Grant; his wife, Lin; and Bob Garthwaite wanted to drive back out to Mineral Wells to a Holiday Inn to show me something. When we arrived, the guys began to tell me about the tradition that followed everyone's first solo flight. You must remember being tossed in the hotel pool in your flight suit! There are rotor blades standing upright in the shape of a capital A, with a sign acknowledging the tradition: Under These Rotor Blades Passed the Finest Helicopter Students in the World July 1, 1956-August 16, 1973. Hard to imagine forty-one thousand students from thirty countries having been slung into that pool! I was surprised the blades were still there, considering it is now 1998. Tom and Bob laughed as they told stories of this-one and that-one being thrown into the pool. I was glad they took me there to see it.

The last evening was the annual banquet. I didn't wear pink (pink for Pink Panthers last year). This year, I wore purple. And I wasn't caught off guard like I had been last year when they began the Missing Man Table ceremony. Still emotional and so well done.

The entertainment after the banquet was none other than Eric Burden of The Animals. I danced a lot and had a great time. What I really want to tell you is how I had no idea at all about what was considered your—meaning you guys in Vietnam—theme song. I found out that night, and I must have been the only one on the planet who didn't know. When Eric Burden began to play *We Gotta Get Outta This Place*, everyone in the entire room—one-thousand-plus, fifty-something-year-old guys—were on their feet. If they weren't dancing, they were singing. Burden sang that song for twenty-five minutes! It was a real eye-opener. I'll never forget the energy in that room that evening, it was palpable.

> *We gotta get out of this place,*
> *If it's the last thing we ever do.*
> *We gotta get out of this place,*
> *Girl there's a better life for me and you.*

I took a hundred pictures at this reunion. I met Harold Goldman, the guy you had been shot down with for the first time. I enjoyed my conversation with Major Rodgers and the others. I can honestly say, without doubt, I have never been around such gentlemen. Never once did anyone enter the elevator in front of me, it was always *after* me. It was the same on escalators, revolving doors, and bus-loading. I am amazed at what I have missed in my forty-plus years. You would be proud of the way these guys have treated me, and the respect they have shown. They are the best bunch of guys in the world!

I know you would have been just like them. Enjoying a beer, bringing the house down with *We Gotta Get Outta This Place*, and always politely waiting while the ladies got on the elevator first. I appreciate them letting me be a part of all this, but I know you would have loved these reunions. These really are your reunions. I think you are with me in spirit, because I feel like this is the right thing to do.

I retraced your steps a little on this trip. Fort Wolters is where you first flew a helicopter, where you were thrown into the pool at the Holiday Inn. I walked on the field at Fort Wolters looking at the static display of helicopters of the Vietnam War. I know you walked on that same field. Maybe you marched there in formation.

I sat on the steps of the stage where your dances were held, while talking to Gary Thewlis about being a committee member. I looked out at the empty hardwood dance floor and imagined it full of uniformed men and dolled up women complete with white gloves and hats. I pictured you and Sherry Davis dancing.

The base is closed now. Fences with concertina wire surround some of the barracks. Void of people and the sound of helicopters above. Time marches on.

Since losing you I never realized how much I didn't know. Seems almost daily there is another small piece of the puzzle I can add. It is never about how you died, though. It is always about how you lived. And for that, I am grateful to the guys of your unit.

Rest in Peace Mark—the guys have your back.

Love, Susie

"In normal life, you have to take some overt action to die. You have to kill yourself. As a prisoner of war, the truth is reversed. You have to reach deep within yourself and struggle each day to stay alive. Dying is easy. Just relax, give up and peacefully surrender, and you will die. Many did."

—Col. William Reeder, Ph. D.,Colonel, U.S. Army (retired) Former POW 1972-1973

GRIEF

Dear Mark,

Although I've read there are five stages of grief, I believe everyone deals with the pain differently. The important part, is working through it—however long it takes.

Denial and anger are two of the classic stages of grief. And both of those stages surprised me.

Just when I thought I was doing fine, something happened that made me realize I was not alright—far from it. Four years after you were gone, completely by accident, I caught the televised news coverage of our American Prisoners of War returning. Finally. The mission was called Operation Homecoming.

On February 12, 1973, a C-141 aircraft transported the first forty of 591 newly released prisoners out of Hanoi, North Vietnam. The ones held the longest were the first to leave for America. Floyd James Thompson came home after more than eight years. He was held longer than anyone.

The first plane out carried gaunt, unhealthy-looking men. Each one stepping out of the aircraft stood there briefly, undoubtedly breathing in freedom and savoring the moment they had waited so long for.

I moved closer to the television so I could see better.

I thought one of those POWs was you; I told myself: it could be you! I did the same thing with the next one, and the next. It had been four years since your crash. You would be older, and without proper nourishment, your face might look different.

In my mind, I imagined every one of them could be you. But the phone didn't ring. No telegram came. Surely they would have notified us to say there had been a huge mistake—that you weren't dead after all! You had been a prisoner of war and now you were on your way home!

I never realized I had been in denial for all those years. I never verbalized it, but I must have harbored thoughts there was still a chance you would return. Was it because we had a closed casket? Your body burned so badly that we weren't allowed to see it?

Was I the only one in our family that thought there might have been a mistake?

It took fifty-four planes—over four months—to repatriate all the prisoners. The North Vietnamese still maintaining control, released a small group at a time. Their first stop was Clark Air Force Base in the Philippines for debriefing, medical evaluation, and to be properly fitted with their branch of the service uniform. A few had been carried off the aircraft on stretchers—too ill to walk. They remained at Clark a little longer for medical care.

Then their last leg home was flying to the United States, where they were reunited with their families. A couple of men kissed the ground. Families with welcome-home signs and American flags all had tears of joy.

Mark, I so badly wanted our family to be one of them.

After all the planes returned and the POW's were reunited with their families, only then did the realization set in—you were not one of them; and never would be.

My heart was broken yet again.

The following is difficult to admit, because I have never told anyone. It's my confession.

In a moment of anger, consumed with grief, I destroyed five reel-to-reel tapes I had of you narrating slides and your recorded music. A complete meltdown. I had finally lost all hope that you would ever return. I couldn't imagine ever listening to your voice again. I had to accept all those men came home—and you weren't one of them.

I was eighteen years old.

I cried. I wailed. I destroyed. I spun the tape off the reels until I was surrounded by broken, brown plastic tape. All of it went in the trash, hiding all of the damage I had caused.

Oh, how I wish I hadn't done that. What I would give to have those tapes now. I knew that wasn't all of the tapes and I searched for years hoping to find the rest. The only ones I found and listened to were of Opa Locka Airport tower communication with airplanes, and more music.

Several times your Army buddies have asked if anyone still has any of the recordings you had made. I told them the truth, no; and leave out the rest of the story.

I have felt horrible—for years—because of what I did that day.

Then twenty-five years later the memory of Operation Homecoming made me feel awful again, but for a different reason.

Let me explain. It was spring, 1998, in Silverdale, Washington, and I had lunch with a man who had been on one of those planes from Hanoi in 1973. COL Bill Reeder was a Pink Panther, like you. He and his co-pilot, Lieutenant Tim Conry, were shot down on May 9, 1972. An explosion occurred shortly after they crashed. They both climbed out of the burning Cobra, but Lieutenant Conry died later that day from his injuries. Bill, injured and alone, managed to avoid capture for three days. When finally caught, the North Vietnamese tortured, interrogated, and offered no medical care.

Yet, when we sat down, it was not his experience and his past that was foremost in his mind. He told me about the missions the Pink Panthers flew. He wanted to answer my questions about what it was like for you in Vietnam. Bill made it clear, though, that I could ask him anything—even about his eleven months of captivity. But I didn't.

How kind this man was to me. Deep inside I felt horrible about the anger I had in 1973, when you had not been among the men on the planes. I should have been thrilled for their release, their freedom, and for the reunions they had.

Bill Reeder arrived at the 361st after you were gone. He was on his second tour in Vietnam, having flown the Grumman OV-1 Mohawk in his first tour. I think you would have loved to have flown one of those airplanes! I got online later that day after meeting Bill and read about the day he was shot down. I read about his broken back, crushed vertebrae and having to carry heavy, uncooked rice—in a rucksack on his back—up the Ho Chi Minh trail, ten hours a day for three months. His captors took his blood-soaked socks and, for whatever reason, the laces off his boots. The lack of treatment for his ankle and leg wounds nearly resulted in amputation right there in the jungle. Infection from his wounds caused his leg to swell, at least double in size, darkened and filled with pus. The skin, taut from swelling, formed cracks... puss and infection oozed out of the cracks. Leeches, no medical care, bamboo cages...I felt awful that I had had any other feeling but joy for him to return to his wife, two children, and his parents. It brings tears to my eyes even now.

I know I wasn't angry he returned. I was angry that you didn't.

Some people say they have no regrets. I guess that's a good place to be later in life—without regret. I have one however, those tapes.

Yet, while I may not be able to hear your voice anymore...

Nothing can ever take you out of my heart.

Love, Susie
p.s. You would really like Bill. I'm sorry you two never met.

I have in a long life known good and brave men but none better, braver, nor more committed than our servicemen in the far east. They are our dearest and our best and more than that— they are our hope.

—John Steinbeck,
Steinbeck in Vietnam: Dispatches from the War.

AIR MEDAL WITH "V"

Dear Mark,

On December 1ˢᵗ, 1968, less than three months after arriving in Vietnam, you were awarded an Air Medal with "V" device. "V" was for valor (or heroism) and this Air Medal was the second Oak Leaf Cluster, meaning this was your third Air Medal. None of which I understood in the early years after your death.

Reading the General Orders only shows a glimpse of how harrowing it must have been that day.

...while serving as pilot/gunner of an AH-1G helicopter in support of a Special Forces reconnaissance team being inserted into an area occupied by enemy battalion. When the lift ship began receiving enemy fire he placed his ship between the slicks and the enemy positions, but one slick was hit and crashed amidst the enemy. Observing enemy soldiers moving in on the downed crew, he immediately began close-in attacks that enabled a chase ship to land and pick up the crew. With complete disregard for his own safety, he pressed the attack under enemy fire until his ship was struck by a 37mm round, causing loss of engine power. He aided the aircraft commander in initiating emergency procedures and in locating a touchdown area. Once safely on the ground, he secured an area just to the front of his downed aircraft and began firing upon

the enemy with his individual weapon. Warrant Officer Clotfelter continued firing until another aircraft extracted him. His actions were in keeping with the highest traditions of the military service and reflect great credit upon himself, his unit, and the United States Army.

Really? You were shot down covering an insertion, had to shoot your own pistol for survival, and you were only awarded an Air Medal? Okay, it had the "V" device for *valor*. Making it better than just an Air Medal. But seriously.

Well, those who did the rescue when you were on the ground probably were awarded something higher like a Distinguished Flying Cross. And rightfully so.

Just looking at your Air Medal sure doesn't tell much of the story. Reading the General Orders and, of course, talking to the ones who were there that day really does tell more of what was behind that medal. Being there, in that moment, whether it was Harold Goldman, your aircraft commander, or Gary Higgins flying as your wingman, they were able to tell me what happened first hand. I hear it in their voices and it's in full color.

When I initially spoke to Harold in 1997, he told me the story. Reminding me you were young and new in-country. He said when you two were shot down, you both grabbed your guns and quickly climbed out of the Cobra. You very seriously asked him if you should set up the perimeter. He chuckles a little and says he told you: "Mark, we ARE the perimeter." He also said you two laughed a little about that and then quickly focused on the severity of the matter, returning fire in several directions.

Occasionally, Gary tells this story at the reunions. He said you guys made a hard landing in very high, razor sharp elephant grass, on a sand bar. A Huey from the 170th Assault Helicopter Company (the Bikini's), went in and picked you guys up.

Went in, in civilian terms, meant flying into a very hostile situation to pick up men they didn't even know, risking their own lives.

Picked up, meaning rescued! Gary added, as soon as you were safely out of there, your helicopter was shot up so the NVA could not get the radios, or anything else that could be useful from U.S. military equipment. He always ends this story with, "Everyone got out alive and without creating a capture or evade-and-escape situation." He tells the story well, like it was yesterday.

I can't imagine how frightening that situation was, wondering if you would get out of there safely. Wondering if you would have enough ammunition to keep the enemy at bay.

Harold Goldman took a photo of the burning Cobra on the sandbar, once he was aboard the Bikini ship with you. I look at the picture now, and know in my heart how that day could have turned out so different.

One of your own slides shows you sitting on the floor of a Huey. It could have been that day. I know your favorite seat in any helicopter would have been the pilot's seat. But looking at the slide of you on the floor of the Huey, I know you were grateful and glad to sit anywhere but the elephant grass.

I understand that oak leaf cluster now.

Love, Susie

Sherry, Sherry baby
She - e - e-e-e-e-ry baby
She - e - rry, can you come out tonight
She - e - e-e-e-e-ry baby
She - e - rry, can you come out tonight
(Why don't you come out) to my twist party
(Come out) Where the bright moon shines
(Come out) We'll dance the night away
I'm gonna make-a you mi-yi-yi-yine
—**Franki Valli and the Four Seasons**

SHERRY

Dear Mark,

Since they built The Wall in D.C. in 1982, I have wanted people to know you were more than *just* a name etched in
that black granite. After Nida gave me the computer, I found
I could post something on the Virtual Wall online... for all
the world to see! I posted your picture and a little about you.
I hoped it would be a reminder for those that knew you, to
not forget you. And also for those that never knew you, to see
you as a *person* and know your dying was a tremendous loss to
those who knew and loved you. This is what I posted under
your picture:

*Greater Love Hath No Man Than This,
That a Man Lay Down His Life, For His Friend.
John 15:13*

*Mark loved sports cars, the Beach Boys, photography, Jan &
Dean, The Ventures, playing chess, flying, and Sherry. Mark,
our only brother, is not just a name on The Wall—he was
a son, a brother, a friend, a cousin, a nephew, an uncle, a
brother-in-law, and a fine pilot.*

Mark began his tour in Vietnam on September 25, 1968. He was assigned to the 361ˢᵗ Aviation Company Escort—the Pink Panthers. Stationed at Camp Holloway in the Central Highlands his unit flew support for SOG (Studies and Observations Group) a joint service, highly classified, unconventional, clandestine operation. These missions were dangerous and demanding for both the ground elements and the supporting air assets. The 361ˢᵗ flew support for teams being inserted along the Cambodian and Laotian borders. These teams were from the 5ᵗʰ Special Forces based in Kontum.

Mark flew the AH-1G Cobra Helicopter for nine months. During this time he was shot down twice before being Killed-In-Action. On a mission not normally flown by the 361ˢᵗ, Mark as Aircraft Commander and Warrant Officer Michael Mahowald as pilot, were shot down by hostile fire while scouting a remote highway needed for a convoy of much needed supplies.

Besides wanting people to know you were more than just a name on The Wall, I was also hoping that if someone saw what I had written online, *and they knew you,* they might contact me. But at the same time I feared Mike Mahowald's family might have thought you were responsible, because you were Aircraft Commander the day that you were shot down. I just didn't know, but I was hoping someday to learn more about Mike Mahowald, the man you died with.

I also hoped for Sherry Davis to see it someday. A woman I wished I had met.

I knew you met Sherry when you were stationed at Fort Wolters Army base in Mineral Wells, Texas in 1967. You wrote me about Texas Woman's University, thirty miles away in Denton, Texas. You told me they were the source for dancing partners on base. Once a month on a Saturday night, the college would load up a bus full of women, all dressed to the nines— complete with white gloves, bus them in, and later, bus them back home. That's how you met Sherry. She was a cute brunette, with a short bob haircut, parted on the side. From your slides I knew you had taken a lot of pictures of her. Picnics, movies, and dances on base. Rereading your letters and looking at her pictures so much over the years—I felt like I knew her. When you left Texas and moved to your next helicopter training at Fort Rucker in Enterprise, Alabama, you started writing to Sherry. When you moved to Savannah, Georgia for training in the Cobra attack helicopter, you continued to write her and then from Vietnam. So, I knew she was special to you.

My heart sinks when I think of how Sherry wasn't included in anything after you died. Of course now when I think about it, there wasn't much to be included in. Even I didn't go to Miami International Airport to meet the plane carrying your casket. And the funeral was just our family. No outsiders except that Marine who stood next to his flag draped casket. No graveside service.

I recently learned from your military records the Military Escort, Jay V. Aliffi attended the memorial service. I am sorry to say I didn't notice him. Maybe he stayed in the back. Once I learned of your escort's name I tried to locate him, believing it is never too late to thank those who cared for you in your final days. I was not successful due to finding on the Internet he had already passed away.

Daddy released your ashes several miles off the coast of Florida, over the Atlantic Ocean, from his own airplane. A private moment, your last flight, just father and son.

Now when I think back, that sinking feeling I got when I thought of Sherry not being included in anything, was also about me not being included in everything.

In 1998, I mentioned to Jack Taber, how someday I would like to find the woman you met and fell in love with in Texas. Jack's sister-in-law was a graduate from Texas Woman's University and he thought she might have an alumni directory. In a few hours he called with her number. I had thought of Sherry so many times over the years, and now I finally had her phone number. I wasn't sure what I would to say to her, but I called anyway.

I introduced myself to her and was immediately thankful she was receptive to the idea of talking to me. I began with, every time, for the past thirty years, when I heard the Four Seasons song *Sherry*, I thought of her. She was pleasantly surprised to hear that. We talked for over an hour. She told me about the last box she had shipped overseas to you, containing orange marshmallow Circus Peanuts. They had been "returned to sender, undeliverable." She also told me about when daddy called her and in a prosaic tone to inform her you had died in Vietnam. It had been an extremely short phone call and she was left to grieve and come to terms with your death with no closure, except the beat up box that had bounced around the Army and the United States Postal Service for so long the Circus Peanuts had dehydrated. Sherry didn't know our parents, and had no way of knowing how they were, or weren't, handling their own raw grief or how they couldn't possibly deal with hers.

Sherry had gone on with her life, graduated, married, still lived in Texas, but assured me she had not forgotten you. She had seen The Traveling Wall, a half scale portable replica of the granite memorial in Washington, D.C. when it came to Texas. She had touched your name and made a pencil etching. She genuinely seemed pleased that I had called and I was appreciative she had not forgotten you. In my heart of hearts, I always felt you would have married her, had you returned from Vietnam. But I think a little part of me had hoped that maybe, just maybe, she could have been pregnant and there would still be a part of you alive somewhere. Maybe I just watch too many movies.

The radio stations seem to play it less and less as the years go by, but I know I will always think of Sherry and you every time I hear *Sherry* by the Four Seasons.

Love, Susie

There is a discipline in a soldier, you can see it when he walks.
There is an honor in a soldier, you can hear it when he talks.
There is a courage in a soldier you can see it in his eyes.
There is a loyalty in a soldier that he will not compromise.

—**Unknown**

MAJOR RODGERS

Dear Mark,

Your first commanding officer in Vietnam, Major Jim Rodgers, was highly respected by everyone who served with him. I heard that first-hand from the guys in your unit in 1997 at the reunion I went to in Orlando.

But before the reunion, I was fortunate to have had a phone conversation with MAJ Rodgers. I asked him about the carbon copy I had of an Application for Appointment he had written on your behalf. He explained it was his recommendation for a Direct Commission or Battlefield Commission for you—stopped in the process by your death.

I looked online to research a Battlefield Commission in Vietnam and a web site said between 1963 and 1973 only sixty-two enlisted men received a commission, including one who was killed before he could accept his. Noting also there had been over 25,000 during World War II. It explained a Battlefield Commission's purpose was to promote enlisted personnel and warrant officers to commissioned officer status, without attending Officer Candidate School. Unfortunately, I can't find a statistic on how many Warrants were promoted like this.

Here is what MAJ Rogers had to say about you:

Part II Statement, 3. Remarks—*Warrant Officer Clotfelter demonstrates maturity and sincerity far beyond his age and experience level. He has rapidly mastered concepts and techniques, and has become an unusually effective* *helicopter gunship and fire team commander. He has achieved outstanding results as a dedicated, aggressive combat leader. He has been repeatedly assigned to unusually hazardous missions in an extremely hostile area, and continues to provide praiseworthy combat support. He has many times been required to make decisions affecting the lives of his own personnel and of supported ground personnel. He has invariably applied sound judgment in reaching reasonable solutions. His aircraft was on one occasion shot down in extremely hostile territory during a very hostile situation. His actions in this situation contributed to the successful culmination of the mission without loss of personnel. He continues to develop as a valuable, potential commissioned officer. I will be pleased to serve with him in that capacity.*

Robert J. Rodgers
MAJ, ARTY
Commanding

Wow! The guys called you serious, yet MAJ Rodgers said you were mature and sincere. Was that essentially the same thing? Reading this makes me proud because it says so much about your character and, possibly, what direction you might have had in life had you not died. You probably would have made a career of the Army and been a great instructor, teaching new pilots combat techniques. You sure had found your niche, and it didn't take MAJ Rodgers long to see it. I know in your short nine months in Vietnam, there were men that returned home to a normal American-way-of-life *because of you.* You were there when they needed you the most.

I am so proud of you.

You may have missed this promotion MAJ Rodgers felt you deserved. But in my book, you were and always will be tops!

Yours, (how *you* used to sign the letters you wrote to me)
Susie

Tach it up, tach it up
Buddy gonna shut you down
It happened on the strip where the road is wide
Two cool shorts standin' side by side
Yeah, my fuel injected Stingray and a 413
We're revvin' up our engines and it sounds real mean
Tach it up, tach it up
Buddy gonna shut you down
—Shut Down by The Beach Boys '64

DADDY AND YOU

Dear Mark,

People have occasionally asked me about you and Daddy. "Were they close?"

You being the only boy, you probably did spend more one-on-one time with Daddy during your teenage years. When you got your driver license it seemed like you two were dragging one junker after the other home. There wasn't any money for a new car. Not for Daddy and Mother or anyone else. It was the same by the time I was old enough to get a car. We were all just happy to have something to drive. Happier when we got in it to go somewhere and it actually started!

Remember the 1958 red MG? I have a great picture of Daddy, up on a ladder in the backyard, getting ready to hoist the engine out of it. There is a huge beam from one tree to another with the pulleys. You're in the picture too, doing something under the dashboard, sitting in the driver's seat. I am guessing this might have been 1964, but there isn't a date on the edge or back of the picture.

I know you got the red MG into great shape, because you drove it to school and I know Redina ended up with it. Not sure when, but it may have been when you enlisted and bought the VW van. The van was more practical for your travels with the Army and all your stuff, but the MG sure was sporty. Redina liked it. Come to think of it, she and Mike also ended up with your van when you left for Vietnam. They told me they had to trade it in on something that could actually make it up the hills when Mike was stationed at Andrews Air Force Base in Virginia.

I was never lucky enough to get a cool hand-me-down car. My first car came from a used car lot—don't think any of yours did. Yours always needed a lot of work, which you and Daddy were capable of doing, from replacing engines to replacing fenders. That way you got a better (cooler) car. I also remember your Austin Healy, a1950-something black panel truck, and a three-wheel motorcycle. Were there two MG's? Redina and Nida think so. Some things are harder to remember.

We only had American, English and German cars, though. Daddy never forgave the Japanese for the bombing of Pearl Harbor. He never spent a dime on a car made in Japan.

Seeing that picture of Daddy in the backyard reminds me of a different engine. You remember the green '55 Buick, the one with one white fender? Was that the engine that we buried in our backyard—because it was easier to bury it than to transport it to the junk-yard? All of us kids—out there in a big circle with shovels—dug the hole to dispose of the large, unwanted, eight-cylinder car engine. I wonder what the neighbors thought.

There are plenty of agencies that would frown on that now, especially the EPA, but I think the statute of limitations would have run out by now.

I've always said there was the right way, the wrong way, and Daddy's way of doing things!

Sure hope no one ever tries to dig a hole for a swimming pool in the backyard on 60th Street.

Many good memories. And you are in all of them!

Love, Susie

> I pray God that our children and their children through all the years to come, will never forget to pay tribute to the gallant men who went fearlessly to their death.
>
> —Mattie Harris Lyons 1850-1947
> Caretaker of Confederate soldiers graves

FROM THE WHITE HOUSE

Dear Mark,

No one wants to receive a letter from the White House like the one Mother and Daddy got in August 1969. I've kept it all these years and often wondered if it was a form letter sent to more than 58,000 families who lost a loved one during the long fourteen-year war. Did our government have a form letter that necessitated that they only fill in the parent's or spouse's name —adding in the appropriate address at the bottom—so all the White House staff had to do was have the President sign it?

Did he ever even read your name?

Dear Mr. and Mrs. Clotfelter:

It is with great sorrow that I have learned of the death of your son, Warrant Officer Mark D. Clotfelter.

Of all the hardships of war, the cruelest are the losses of men such as your son. The only consolation I can offer is the profound respect of the nation he died to serve, and the humble recognition of a sacrifice no man can measure, and no words can describe. Those who give their own lives to make the freedom of others possible live forever in honor.

Mrs. Nixon joins me in extending our own sympathy, and in expressing the sympathy of a saddened nation. You will be in our prayers, and in our hearts.

Sincerely,

Richard Nixon

An obligatory letter, even in the worst of times, was not important enough for Daddy to hold on to. I've had the letter since 1973, when we sold the house in Hialeah; Mother and Daddy didn't include it in their packed boxes, so I did.

"A saddened nation?" Really? The nation was protesting against the war and seemingly against the soldiers, sailors, airmen and the Marines. The nation was not showing respect for the military—living or dead. No wonder this letter was not important to Mother or Daddy.

Eisenhower was President when the Vietnam War unofficially started in the mid-1950's. In 1961, John F. Kennedy was elected. I had just started first grade.

Gosh, now that I think about it, the war went on the entire time I went to school—and we just lived our lives as if there wasn't a war.

You remember Kennedy's assassination in 1963? Then Lyndon Johnson was sworn in. He was elected to a full term in 1964.

While you were training stateside in 1968—learning to fly helicopters—Johnson was the one who increased combat troops in Vietnam: from 16,000 to over a half-million! That is really when crime in the States increased and war protests spread to so many university campuses.

You were one of those increased combat troops.

This might be a good place to tell you about someone interesting in our family tree. Over the years I learned that Dean Rusk, who was Secretary of State from 1961-1969, was a cousin of ours. His grandfather and our grandfather were half-brothers. I read his autobiography in order to understand his position during the Vietnam War; he was Secretary of State when you were there.

Rusk hated communism and believed using military action was the right thing to do. He also believed the United States could have won the war had they not lost the support of the American people. But what really stood out to me was how he and Kennedy disagreed regularly. Because of that, Rusk tried to resign more than once and those resignations were refused by Kennedy and later by Johnson. Rusk's last resignation was offered for personal reasons—what he called a "family matter." He believed his daughter Peggy's marriage in 1967, to a black classmate at Stanford University, would cause embarrassment to the White House. President Johnson refused to accept the resignation, and Rusk walked his daughter Peggy down the aisle and served to the end of his term in 1969. The wedding was national news, coming on the heels of the civil rights movement and the end of segregation. It was featured in Time magazine and our local papers, The Miami Herald and The Miami News.

I recently learned that Peggy's husband, Guy Gibson Smith, a highly respected officer in the Army, became a helicopter pilot, Class 69-12. He served in Vietnam and flew with the 162nd Attack Helicopter Company in 1969 and 1970. When I asked his commanding officer, Ken Loveless, if he remembered Guy, Loveless said he remembered Smith fondly. When Loveless came to the 162nd, Smith was in an administrative job because the commanding officer that preceded Loveless, thought it best the Secretary of State's son-in-law was safer not flying—and certainly not flying combat missions!

After the change of command Loveless put him in a platoon rotation, thus allowing Smith to do what he was trained to do—fly! It wasn't long before…you guessed it! Smith took some shrapnel and a bullet in the arm while out flying a combat mission. Loveless told me how Smith downplayed his wounds—"just a nick," he said. They were minor wounds, but not as minor as Smith was making them out to be!

After his scheduled year-long tour in Vietnam Smith returned home. Their story doesn't end there, though. Peggy and Guy had one daughter, Samantha, and a forty-four-year-long marriage, which ended only by his death in 2012. A wonderful love story that criticism and racism could not destroy.

Enough of our family history…

Mark, Johnson didn't seek reelection. I don't know if it was because he didn't want the humiliation of losing or as James R. Jones wrote in the L.A. Times in 2008, "…he wanted his presidency to be judged well by history. His foreboding was that the war would overshadow all of his domestic accomplishments."

The war probably does overshadow any of the good Johnson was able to accomplish. The deaths on his watch included the single-worst-day of casualties—245 on January 31, 1968. I looked up that date on the Internet to see what I could find about that day in history. I can tell you Judy in Disguise (With Glasses) by John Fred and his Playboy Band was the number one song in the United States. I can tell you January 31, 1968 was a Wednesday. And I can tell you it was during the '68 Tet Offensive, which was one of the largest, bloodiest battles fought during the Vietnam War—huge losses on both sides. But I can't tell you what I was doing. Probably just going to school, hanging out with Lori and looking forward to a dance Friday night at the junior high school. Odd how life was so normal for us in the United States, while war raged on and lives were being lost in battle far away.

Also on Johnson's watch was the single worst month, May 1968, a casualty count of 2,415! Of the eight service women killed in Vietnam, seven of them were killed while Johnson was in office. No doubt Johnson signed more condolence letters while in office than any other president. Not a record to be proud of!

Nixon beat Hubert Humphrey in the election and was propelled into the White House on his promise to end the draft and restore law and order to all the cities with high crime. You were in Vietnam while this was going on—you were kind of busy and may not have been paying too much attention to what was happening in the States!

Later the draft did end. And Nixon ordered the troops out of Vietnam in 1973. But we, as a nation just left the poor South Vietnamese to fend for themselves. After all the lives that were lost and all the damage that was done, we, the United States, just pulled our military out and left. Sadly, we left the South Vietnamese to take whatever retaliation the communist North Vietnamese thrust upon them. I can only imagine how horrible it must have been. Vietnam remains a communist country today.

Turns out, according to the Vietnam Helicopter Pilots Association statistics, out of 40,000 trained pilots, only 559 were black. Sadly, there were 2,097 helicopter pilots lost between 1961 and 1975.

I know veterans who have gone back to Vietnam lately with the Military Historical Tours. They tell me it is truly a beautiful country. After four decades, I guess they see it differently now—without the bombing, and the specter of death.

I would like to go to Vietnam some day. I think about going to the site where you crashed. Not sure how that would feel—not sure what's there now.

Still sure, though—that I miss you every day,

Your little sister,

Susie

MAY 25, 2000

Dear Mark,

You probably don't know about Mother becoming a *Gold Star Mother* when you died. The Gold Star is a round, gold colored pin, with a purple star in the center; given to mothers for the loss of their child in combat. It has the same colors as the Purple Heart Medal you received when you died—and all soldiers receive when they are wounded-in-action. *Almost like it's given to the mother for her broken heart.* Wow, I never thought of it that way before.

There seems to be a fractured system from getting it to the mothers —to the public understanding of it.

I personally never heard of it until 1997, when I began looking for your unit in Vietnam. The guys I met from different organizations referred to Mother as a Gold Star Mom, and me as a Gold Star sister, so I did some research on it. Mother had never received a pin. I didn't know if it should have been included with your medals that were presented to Mother and Daddy, or just mailed to her by the government.

It wasn't until 1999 when I mentioned it to a retired Colonel, Mike Sloniker, and he suggested I contact my congressman to accelerate the process to get Mother's much over-due Gold Star. So I did. For two months, correspondence was exchanged between me, my Congressman Jay Inslee's office in Washington State and the National Personnel Records Center, in St. Louis, Missouri. By then I had heard everyone in the family was entitled to a Gold Star but I was only interested in getting Mother's—already thirty years late!

When Congressman Inslee's office called to say they had received it, I was elated. They wanted to present it to me, and I reminded them that it was for my seventy-eight-year-old mother who lived in Maryland. Still, we agreed on a time and I suggested my aunt and uncle's house for this little "presentation" the next day. Seemed appropriate. Aunt Arlene and Uncle Coston were the last ones you visited on your way to Vietnam—my surrogate parents with Daddy gone and Mother living so far away. Uncle Coston, a World War II vet, was pleased I included them.

I came straight from work and Mr. Inslee and his aide (camera in tow) arrived on time. I expressed appreciation for Mr. Inslee's staffs' effort, and also acknowledged it may have taken me years—and at Mother's age I didn't know if she had years. Mr. Inslee remarked at how young and brave you had been and his added apologies for the government not getting the pin to Mother years ago. I thanked him and told him I would hand it to Mother as soon as I could.

When I spoke with Mike Sloniker about congressman Inslee getting Mother's Gold Star pin he told me about the book, The Price of Exit, by Tom Marshall. I picked it up that weekend and read it all afternoon. On page 355, I stopped and read this paragraph three times:

> "*The Bureaucracy in place during and after the war years provided minimal acknowledgment of the family losses. Little or no help was proffered, or interest expressed after the funerals: a short ceremony, a purple heart, a flag, and a Gold Star pin, and that was all. They were left on their own to grieve and reconcile their feelings.*"

Here it was decades later and finally Mother was getting her pin—finally.

The Gold Star is modest and unpretentious. Those who recognize it know Mother wears the pin because she lost a child in combat. My guess is there will be many that won't have a clue what it is. Vietnam veterans will know and all seem to hold these Gold Star Mothers in very high regard. *I think it's because they know it could very easily have been their own mother.*

I still don't understand why Mother was never given her Gold Star in 1969 or even in 1970 when the medals were presented to our parents. She never would have joined other Gold Star Mothers in ceremonies or events that they sometimes participate in. Her loss is private and probably unhealthy. Still keeping it all in—all these years.

Now, just this year, I too, wear a Gold Star to honor you. When I requested one from the government they said I had already received one and was not entitled to another. I tried to explain that the one I had previously requested was for Mother—twelve years ago. It's hard to cut through the red tape with letters, so I requested assistance from Governor Nathan Deal's office. They were happy to help. It took a few months but it arrived in a very small, brown, bubble envelope. If the office that sent it knew what it stood for or what it meant to me, maybe it could have arrived in something a little more official. The package looked more like I purchased a guitar pin from Hard Rock Café!

While waiting for the pin to arrive, I decided to have the pin made into a pendant. As soon as I received it, I took it to the jeweler who had no idea what the pin was. He required me to sign a waiver in case it melted, because the loop to be attached to the top was real gold, but the pin itself is not. Thankfully it didn't melt and turned out beautiful!

Also, my Georgia license tag is now a Gold Star Family tag. I have never seen another one in a parking lot or on the road. I think that's a good thing. I would hope the state never has to issue too many of them—each one representing a loss in combat.

The forms the motor vehicle department required to verify your loss were not even used during the Vietnam War. It appeared I may have been the first one ever to come to this office for a Gold Star Plate because of a combat death so long ago. They had never seen such old documents! I brought more than enough for them to choose from. After a few phone calls and photocopies they accepted "Notification of Death" and the 1969 obituary that verified me as your sister.

It's too late for Daddy. I don't know if he would have even worn the Gold Star on his lapel the few times during the year he wore a suit. He could have worn it on the VFW hat he wore on occasion. Somehow, I don't think he would have wanted to answer a question like "What does that pin signify?"

Love,
Your Gold Star Sister—something I wish I didn't qualify for,
Susie

Sometimes I feel my heart is breaking
But I stay strong and I hold on cause I know
I will see you again, ohhh
This is not where it ends
I will carry you with me, yeah yeah.
I'll see you again.

—Carrie Underwood

NOVEMBER 29, 2001

Dear Mark,

Have you ever gone somewhere—that you *really* had to drag yourself to, but once you got there, you were glad you made the effort? Regarding what I am about to tell you, glad is probably not the word—thankful is closer to the truth.

I read an announcement in the weekly North Kitsap Herald that a documentary would be shown Thursday night. Letters to the Wall, A Documentary on the Vietnam Wall Experience would be shown at the Undersea Warfare Museum in Keyport, Washington. Immediately, I was interested in going.

After work on Thursday, I rushed home, changed clothes and grabbed a bite to eat. I hadn't been able to find anyone at work to go with me—you know how I hate going anywhere alone! I made one more phone call, to Nida. She turned me down because she gets up so early to drive the school bus. I had struck out all day long trying to get someone to accompany me—including my own sister! The longer I sat, the more tired I got and finally decided I should just skip it.

The drive to Keyport is twenty minutes at most. I reread the article and changed my mind again, deciding to just go! I'm so happy I did.

I parked my car, still wishing I wasn't alone, but headed to the steps near the flagpole. This is a public facility, just outside a military base, so when I saw the black POW/MIA flag hanging under the American flag, I was pleased. The POW/MIA flag is generally not flown on flagpoles not affiliated with the military. The Post Office is the exception. It's a reminder for us not to forget those that never returned from war. It breaks my heart when I think of those parents who have now passed on, those poor souls who never knew the fate of their missing child.

Wes Cary, the film's producer, greeted me on the steps. I introduced myself and I told him about you. I can't remember how it came up, because I don't usually go up to strangers and tell them you were killed in Vietnam. He must have asked me why I had interest in the film.

Mr. Cary introduced me to a Hank Cramer and told him your name is on The Wall. Hank, whose father's name is also on The Wall, soon asked me to join him and his wife, Kit, in the auditorium to watch the film. I felt so welcomed. I knew I had made the right decision to come. I sure didn't feel like I was alone anymore.

The program began, flags were presented, and Hank went up to the stage to sing the National Anthem—a cappella. What a terrific baritone voice! It was a surprise. Hank doesn't even need a microphone!

The lights were dimmed and the film began. "The documentary is not about war, it's not about politics. It's about people... the ones that are here, and the ones who didn't make it back."

Wow, what a powerful beginning.

Hank is in the film also, and I learned he was only three when, in 1957, his father died in Vietnam. Captain Harry Cramer was a Special Forces officer in Vietnam before anyone knew we had advisors there—before there was officially was a Vietnam War.

In the film Hank talks about being so young and losing his father. Later in the film he sings a song called Touch a Name On The Wall. The ending—profound:

Now, usually walls are made for division
To separate me from you.
But God Bless The Wall that brings us together,

And reminds us of what we've been through.
And God damn the liars and the tin-plated heroes who
Trade on the blood of such men.
God give us the strength to stand up and tell them-

Never again!
Touch a name on the Wall
God help us all
Touch a name on The Wall.

Mark, what a night I had. The documentary was so well done. During the reception, following the film, I met Robert Dowling and Susan Welch, both featured in the film. Robert's father was a helicopter pilot with the 197th AHC. I can't imagine what that would have been like to not have Daddy around when we grew up. Susan sang *Touch A Name* with Hank in the film.

I am so glad I didn't bag it and just stay home. I bought the documentary and two patriotic scarves. It turned out to be an evening I will never forget.

Since that night I have seen Hank perform in venues around Seattle, singing mostly folk music. Mike and I saw him at Folk Life Fest, a Bainbridge Island church, boating festivals where he sings Sea Shanty songs, and in Port Gamble, where we were able to sit and have a beer with him afterwards.

At the twenty-fifth anniversary of the Vietnam Veterans Memorial in 2007, Hank sang the National Anthem. During the four days of reading all the names on The Wall, Hank read his father's name and I read yours. After the Veterans Day Ceremony at the Wall, we took some pictures and then Redina and I had lunch with Hank.

We keep in touch mostly through the internet now, because Mike and I moved to Georgia. I miss seeing Hank perform.

But one day I went to the mailbox and got a nice surprise. He had sent me his new CD called A Soldier's Songs. The next best thing to seeing him perform is listening to his CD's. The cover has Hank in his Class A dress uniform and his green beret. You would love this CD. It has one of your favorites: The Ballad of the Green Beret.

What I forgot to mention is that Hank followed in his dad's footsteps. He served with the elite 1st Special Forces Group (Airborne) serving all over the world. His entire career was spent in service to our country.

I have been so blessed with the people I have met—all because of you. There must be some metaphor for the wonderful people who have come into my life because of having lost you. But I can't think of any.

I would rather have you back—in a heartbeat—but know that's not ever going to be possible. So I count my blessings for the people like Hank Cramer who came into my life because of you. And there are so many like Hank who I have met since 1997. These people have not come into my life for just the moment or the event—I know they came into my life for a reason. Divine guidance? Maybe.

I don't question the why's too much. I just know I am in a better place now that the Vietnam War is out of the closet!

Talking about losing you and meeting others who experienced this same loss, whether it was a brother or a father, has proven to be better than holding it all in. I wish I had not waited twenty-eight years to get started.

Love, Susie

Susan, I went over just before Mark. I flew many times with him and got to know him well. He was a much better pilot than I was. I have always felt sad for those whose life ended so early. Mark loved life........

—Frank Waugh

NINE LIVES

Dear Mark,

Part luck, part skill—whatever you call it, it was bound to run out.

When I tell someone the last year of your life was action-packed, I mean it. When Gary Higgins, your comrade-in-arms, tells a story that you are in, he usually mentions: "Mark was like a cat with nine lives." I thought about Gary saying that, more than once. So I started jotting down incidents. You know—he was right!

However, it started before you and Gary even went to Vietnam.

Remember when you were helping Daddy on that job-site on Miami Beach, and the circular saw you were using hit a knot or something and ended up on your thigh? Daddy took you to the hospital, called Mother and said, "Mark has a little scratch and is getting stitches."

Little scratch? Stitches? That little scratch was about nine inches long, who knows how deep, and required you to be in an aluminum splint to stabilize your leg for weeks! I know, that wasn't exactly a nine-lives kind of moment, but seriously scary for sure. Several months later when you went for your Army physical, your leg was still red where it had been stitched. They asked you if it bothered you and your reply was "not at all."

If you had ever wanted an excuse for staying out of the Army, you could have used that! Not that it ever entered your mind

Then there was the time when you had just earned your pilot license, rented a Cessna 150, and started taking people up for a twenty-minute ride. First Daddy, then Nida, and last was Dennis. After leaving the runway—still climbing and probably about five-hundred feet up—Dennis asked you where he could adjust the seat to get more leg room. You were busy, hands on the wheel, and never looked down; you pointed between the seats with your pinky and said, "down there." Moments later, the propeller stopped straight up and down. You immediately called "Mayday, Mayday!" The tower responded and instructed you to turn one-hundred-eighty-degrees and land on the taxiway you had just left.

You landed dead-stick!

After dinner and discussion of what could possibly have caused the engine to quit so suddenly, you and Daddy came to the conclusion: Dennis must have shut off the fuel valve. You and Daddy hopped in the car and returned to the airport, located the rental airplane where it had been towed, and looked between the seats. Indeed, the fuel lever was in the "off" position.

Okay, now we get into Vietnam. October 6, 1968—in-country for only eleven days:

The enemy was within 25 meters of the friendly position, and because of heavy automatic weapons fire, slicks had been unable to extract the patrol. Warrant Officer Clotfelter arrived and began a series of firing runs upon the enemy positions. Despite receiving heavy automatic weapons fire on each pass, he continued to place suppressive fire within 20 meters of the patrol until an extraction became feasible. While the patrol was being lifted from the area on McGuire Rigs, suspended from a UH-1H helicopter, he flew at tree-top level to divert enemy fire, due to the fact that his ship had already received several hits. Warrant Officer Clotfelter's courageous, skilled performance greatly abetted the successful extraction of the patrol and inflicted heavy losses upon the enemy...

I read between the lines of what happened and know darn well there could easily have been a different outcome during this extraction! Later, you were awarded your first Distinguished Flying Cross for what you did that day.

Are you counting? I would say that's three. Stay with me, there's more!

December 1, 1968, you and Harold Goldman were shot down. You had to use your own personal weapons for survival, and luckily were picked up by the Bikinis, the 170th Assault Helicopter Company, and taken back to Dak To. Unfortunately, the Cobra helicopter you left in the elephant grass had to be shot up so the North Vietnamese Army would not gain anything from it.

That's four!

Gary and you were flying together again on December 19. Same day, same mission, when Ben Ide was lost. Paul Renner and Ben were shot up and had to be picked up by the Bikinis. Your aircraft was hit, the six-inch hole under Gary's seat and the wiring harness that was hanging and smoking were only part of the damage. Somehow you were able to get back across the border and land at Dak To. The Cobra was too badly damaged to repair.

That was a sad day for the Panthers—losing Ben Ide. You and Gary were shot up too and that makes five.

January 27th, 1969, during the Vietnamese Tet holiday, there should not have been any activity from the NVA. However, intelligence from the radio relay station, Leghorn, warned of large troop and truck movement.

You, Gary Higgins, and Paul Renner were launched in a mission to provide cover for insertion of troops into a Landing Zone. Along the Dak Xou River, paralleling Route 110, you and Gary were bombarded by a hail of gunfire. Hundreds of enemy troops stood up in the high grass below and fired small arms directly at you! You and Gary were hit—the Cobra shook awkwardly and it sounded like "beating on a base drum with a baseball bat." You were firing everything you had back at the enemy, while Gary tried to maintain control of the badly damaged helicopter. Streaming white vapor, Paul Renner flew up beside you after you had distanced yourselves from the enemy, and radioed that your skids looked broken. Gary told Paul to "drop back in case the Cobra broke up—or suddenly blew up."

My God—that gives me goose bumps!

Gary shut off all electronics, for fear it would spark the leaking fuel. You were using hand signs and shouting to each other about how you were going to do the landing, when suddenly a Sky Raider appeared saying he "would stay with you until you either went down or made it to base."

More goose bumps!

With your visibility distorted and the ten-percent fuel warning light on, you guys made a hard landing back at Dak To. Your eyes "burning from fuel vapor," you both quickly released your harnesses and body armor and jumped out of the Cobra, running through heavy fuel mist coming off the still moving rotor blades. All the guys who had heard of your trouble and had come out to the runway ran too!

When it appeared the danger of fire had passed, you and Gary retrieved your personal weapons and gear. The foaming crew arrived and was thoroughly surprised that "all the fuel that leaked out did not ignite a fireball."

Later after examining the Cobra Gary said, "We were lucky the airframe and transmission had not separated in flight!"

I don't think I can even imagine how scary that must have been.

Now we are up to six.

On April 7, 1969, you were lead gunship and mission commander on a much needed resupply mission into a company-sized unit which was badly in need resupply and medical aid across the border into Laos. Two aircraft had previously been shot down trying to land. This is what your Distinguished Flying Cross General Orders said:

...escorting the first cargo aircraft into the landing zone, placing suppressive rocket and minigun fire on reported

enemy positions. As he was escorting the first cargo helicopter into the landing zone, his ship received heavy ground fire from automatic weapons. Warrant Officer Clotfelter quickly suppressed the enemy positions with rocket fire. He elected to stay with his fire team and protect the remaining aircraft as they landed in the landing zone. Again the fire team came under attack and his aircraft received more battle damage. After being assured another gunship team was on station. Warrant Officer Clotfelter executed a pinnacle approach to a mountain 20 kilometers away, which saved the aircraft from being destroyed...

You were shot up so badly, causing a loss of oil pressure and very low on fuel, you were forced to make a landing on Leghorn. No easy task with your helicopter damaged, as Leghorn is on a ridge top, one thousand feet above the valley floor with almost vertical sides, in the Attapeu Province of Laos. The landing pad itself was so narrow it only had space for the skids, leaving the nose and tail hanging over the edge.

Still receiving enemy fire from the base of the mountain, a Gladiator gunship with the 57th Assault Helicopter Company was able to rescue you, with wingman Al Porter providing the firepower to complete the pickup. Porter barely made it back to Dak To on the little fuel he had left! I don't think you ever knew that you were awarded a Distinguished Flying Cross that day... you died sixty-nine days later, and the military just doesn't move that fast.

That makes seven.

Number eight would be your final-shoot down on June 16, 1969. The one that still breaks my heart. You didn't quite make it to the old cliché—the cat with nine lives.

Your Distinguished Flying Cross certificate, the one embossed in a padded binder simply states: For Heroism while participating in Aerial Flight in Vietnam on 16 June 1969

That sure doesn't tell the story. I tried to find the usual paperwork that goes with it, but I can't. I've searched through everything. I'm not sure I ever had it. It's possible I only thought I had it because I have several that say General Orders at the top of the page. The General Orders would tell the military version, but I have the real version. I have the eyewitness version of Alan Porter, who was flying closer to you than anyone—he was your wingman.

Porter wrote me that you guys, in separate Cobras, were crisscrossing the road, back and forth. You had just begun the reconnaissance for the truck convoy that was carrying much needed supplies on Highway 512, between Ben Het and Dak To. Porter glanced over and saw you at tree-top level, and the next glance you had disappeared. Hit by small arms fire, and then gone. For a moment he thought you just went a little low and you would come back up, but the next thing he saw was a huge ball of fire—then he knew.

In a split second, you were gone.

The story is your helicopter crashed and burned furiously on the bunker the NVA were hiding in when they shot you down. When you and Mahowald were finally retrieved from the aircraft, they found the two NVA bodies in the bunker. Sweet revenge? One might call it that. I would call it avenging your own death.

When I started this letter, it was kind of funny. Daddy saying you had a little scratch—Dennis accidentally turning off the gas in the Cessna, but then every time you barely managed to get back safely, or had to be rescued—it seemed to get more dangerous.

Gotta go now. I was doing okay listing all of this until I got to the end. It's been over forty years and what happened to you still gets to me when I put it on paper or I think about it too much. I'll be okay, I just have to close now.

Still affected by your death, yet inspired by your zest for life,

Your little sister, Susie

In peace, sons bury their fathers.
In war, the fathers bury their sons.

—Herodotus, 425 BC

PINK PANTHERS

Dear Mark,

Hal Manns, a Pink Panther who arrived in Vietnam after you were gone, put together a three-inch, three- ring binder, with the history of your unit. He mailed one to Mother and one to me. It must have taken him years to gather all the information. You should see it! It's so heavy Mother can't even lift it! The details, pictures, maps, and everyone's contributions have made it so complete and factual. Imagine my surprise when I found a few letters of appreciation I had sent over the years thanking the guys for sharing their memories of you with me. Where would I be without their willingness? I'm so glad I found them.

I know you would have done the same for some other "little sister" had you come home.

The history was interesting to read, discovering how the unit was activated November 1, 1967, at Fort Hood, Texas, and arriving in Vietnam on April 6, 1968. They had four months to get themselves and their equipment ready and to prepare their families for their year-long deployment.

Also described are the missions flown by the 361st in Vietnam, Laos and Cambodia. I read they stood down—packed up and returned to the States—in August 1972. I suspect that must have been a bittersweet time for those still in the unit. I'll have to ask some of the guys someday. Happy to be going home, but maybe a little sad the unit itself was shutting its doors—forever.

Many have told me their year in Vietnam was the most exciting year of their life!

You are mentioned many times throughout the history—even though you were only there a short nine months. Like when you received awards, actions you were in and when you were shot down, all three times.

There's list of those killed with the 361st. Only eight. Ben Ide was the first loss. Then you and Mike Mahowald. Larry Brown and Francis Monroe, both maintenance men who went out in the dark of night, in a jeep, to pick up two men stranded in Pleiku—knowing the danger yet went anyway, and then they were ambushed. Alejandro Makintaya and Michael Kilduff were out on a maintenance flight, crashing after encountering bad weather. And in May of '72, Tim Conry died when he was shot down with Bill Reeder. Reeder was captured three days later and held prisoner until '73.

Those eight names are right in front of me now. Seems odd. In '69 we had no idea who had been with you when you were shot down. Now you can go online to the Department of Defense and find a list of every name of those lost in the current war.

From the Unit Operations section of the History of the 361st:

The 361ˢᵗ Cobras turned many desperate situations into accomplished missions. Regardless of darkness of night, adverse weather conditions or intense enemy fire, if a team was called for extraction—the Pink Panthers responded. Missions included but were not limited to aerial fire support for troops in contact, gun cover for insertion of Special Forces, road convoy coverage and five-minute stand-by for the nightly defense of Camp Holloway and surrounding areas.

Somehow I thought you wouldn't be able to fly in the rain—or the dark. After reading that I see I was wrong.

Today, I ran across the General Orders for the Army Commendation Medal you were awarded. Not just the Army Commendation but with a "V" for valor: November 16, 1968.

...For heroism in connection with military operations against a hostile force: These men distinguished themselves by exceptionally valorous actions while serving as pilot gunners on AH-1G attack helicopters, engaged in escorting a medical evacuation aircraft into a landing zone in which a Special Forces reconnaissance team was in heavy contact with the enemy. An enemy battalion had the reconnaissance team surrounded and was positioned within 300 meters of the landing zone. In spite of the intense anti-aircraft fire, these men identified and engaged the enemy emplacements. On repeated passes against the enemy, they placed accurate fire upon them, thereby facilitating a successful evacuation without loss of friendly personnel...

What I could never imagine as a teenager was just how determined the North Vietnamese Army was to kill our troops on the ground not to mention shooting our helicopters out of the sky—no mercy for the wounded—or for those trying to rescue them.

In an eyewitness statement from by SP/5 James M. Tramel:

On 16 November 1968 I was command-and-control over a medevac mission of a Special Forces reconnaissance team. The team consisted of one hundred-twenty-five men of which a number were wounded. They were surrounded by a battalion of North Vietnamese Army reinforced with 50 caliber and 37mm anti-aircraft weapons. After the evacuation aircraft attempted three times to land and was shot out of the landing zone, the Cobra fire team, which was covering, instructed the evacuation ship to orbit and then started attacking the enemy positions. After they made several passes, the enemy positions were neutralized and the medevac slick was able to land and pick up the wounded. As he was leaving the landing zone a 50 caliber opened up hitting the evac-ship twice before being silenced by the Cobras.

You were in one of those Cobras.

Two days later, November 18, 1968, you have General Orders for an Air Medal (First Oak Leaf Cluster) with "V" Device. Your name and LT Paul Renner are on this, and the reason:

> ... *These men distinguished themselves by exceptionally valorous actions while serving as pilots/gunners of AH-1G gunships in support of a long range reconnaissance team in contact with a large enemy force. They arrived in the target area and placed accurate machine gun and 40mm grenade fire on enemy positions in close proximity to the team. Despite hostile automatic weapons fire directed at them, they continued to place ordnance on enemy positions, until all wounded personnel were safely evacuated. When advised that the remaining members of the reconnaissance team required a night resupply if they were to survive, they voluntarily returned to the area. Despite darkness, mountainous jungle terrain, and the intense enemy fire, they made low firing passes which neutralized enemy fire, thus preparing the way for the resupply aircraft. Their actions were in keeping with the highest traditions of the military service and reflect great credit upon themselves, their unit, and the United States Army.*

Major Rodgers wrote a Letter of Commendation on November 20, 1968:

To: WO1 Mark D. Clotfelter

1. *You can justly be proud of your contributions to the welfare of this gravely-endangered friendly force. Without your assistance, they would surely be overwhelmed by the vastly superior force opposing them.*

2. *I personally observed an earlier display of your gallantry in support of this same force, wherein you made repeated*

attacks against intense heavy weapons fire. Your actions were indeed in keeping with the highest traditions of the military service.

3. *This outstanding performance is but one of many you have rendered in helping to carry out this unit's combat missions. On behalf of the unit and our country, I thank you.*

Robert J. Rodgers
MAJ, ARTY
Commanding

Makes me proud knowing how brave you were—how you helped save those men who so desperately needed medical attention. Or those who needed the night time resupply. I know you didn't do it alone. But you did your part and because you did, there is someone alive, somewhere, that remembers the life-saving heroics of the Cobras.

When I put this in perspective, I am even more stunned—after all you were only twenty-one and you had only been in Vietnam barely two months. I know I am just the little sister, but I find that all pretty awesome!

You will always be pretty awesome to me...

Susie

> Of what shall a man be proud,
> If he is not proud of his friends?
>
> —Robert Louis Stevenson

FRIENDS

Dear Mark,

I have wanted to tell you, for a while now about some of the sweet, kind things people have written to me since 1997, when I began my quest to learn more about you. Most are from people who personally knew you, a few are from people who believed in my mission and were helpful along the way. All of them touched my heart in a way that is hard to describe. Like the e-mail I received from:

JOHN PLUMMER, APRIL 1997 (JOHN PERFORMED OUR MARRIAGE IN 2006)

We're glad you stumbled on our group, The Vietnam Helicopter Flight Crew Network, and pray you'll be able to learn more about Mark through the information you'll receive. Julie has become very special to all of us because her brother was our brother. Same goes for Mark. That makes you a part of our family. Although he's no longer with us in person, his spirit will be with us forever.

JIM WATKINS, SEPTEMBER 1997: RIP JIM!

I arrived in the 361st ACE in August of 1969. I did not get a chance to meet your brother Mark—but I sure did hear about him. Based on his reputation, he was an incredibly fine Cobra pilot and quite a guy. You must be proud of your brother.

MICHAEL JIMISON, JUNE 1997 PANTHER 21
(THE PINK PANTHER I MARRIED IN 2006)

I remember Mark as a dedicated and reliable pilot who was quiet and serious in a crowd of loud and rowdy pilots. I admit that I held my end up in that department. I don't remember Mark ever involved in that but the first few weeks were a blur.

CHARLIE MOUTENOT, SEPTEMBER 1997 PANTHER 34, NOW A JESUIT PRIEST

I knew Mark for only a short time. I remember that when we arrived in-country—Mark was the one you wanted to fly with. He was top-notch. He knew the Area of Operation well and was wise. I also remember him as a moral man, not prudish, but a good solid moral person. I was one of the pounders (drinkers). I never saw Mark act anything but in a gentlemanly and kind way. In that regard he was a challenge to me.

I was invited by Bob Whitford to attend the memorial service for Mark and Mike. I well remember their boots in front of the chapel.

I believe in life after death. I think your brother is looking at you now with tremendous love, pride and happiness. Your father, too. I went back to the website and reread your piece on discovering the Pink Panthers and your poem about the Cobra. It was moving and wonderfully healing.

You and your family remain in my prayers.

ROGER EK, APRIL 1997: A HELICOPTER PILOT OF THE VHFCN

We'll never forget Mark and those like him. We were the first pilots in history who could retrieve one of our own who had been shot down and bring him back into the air. We would have done it for Mark and he would have done it for us.

WAYNE CLARK, AUGUST 1997: FLIGHT SCHOOL CLASSMATE

I was a member of Flight Class 68-9 with your brother. He slept on the lower bunk when we were in the preflight

barracks. Later he had the room next door. After graduation we went our separate ways. I remember he was pretty quiet and he took flying very seriously. Your brother was one of the more mature and one of the nicest guys in our flight class.

BOB WHITFORD, JUNE 16, 1997 PANTHER ON THE ANNIVERSARY OF YOUR DEATH

Thinking of you, your family, and Mark today.

JULIE KINK, JUNE 16, 1997 GOLD STAR SISTER

I hope this day brings you peace. I will be thinking of you. I have the day on my calendar but you have it marked in your hearts

BRAD ARTHUR, MAY 30, 1997 PANTHER

Yes, I certainly do remember Mark. I arrived in Vietnam March 1969 so I only knew him for three months. He gave me my first check-ride when I arrived and if I remember correctly we flew a few missions in Laos together. He could really fly that Cobra.

JACK TABER , APRIL 1997 CLASS MATE 68-9

I admire your efforts in putting Mark's life in perspective for future generations.

RALPH MULLENS, SEPTEMBER 1997 PANTHER

I had the chance to work and socialize with your brother and I can tell you that he was one of the most mature and respected Aircraft Commanders in the 361ˢᵗ. He was extremely professional and would do anything for his fellow country-man. Mark was a wonderful person and will always occupy a special place in my heart.

ALAN PORTER, JANUARY 2006

Mark and I shared the same hooch in Vietnam and flew together almost every day for the last six months. We rotated lead, with Mark being lead one day and I was his wingman, and I would lead the next day with Mark being my wingman.

The 361ˢᵗ was a unique aviation company. I flew for multiple aviation companies in the regular army and reserves and I have found nothing that compared. Every single pilot in the 361ˢᵗ was the best—as a pilot, dedication, professionalism and as a good person. I was honored to be in the company of so many good people. Mark was one of the good guys, my friend and was a great professional pilot.

HARRY SMALL, JUNE 4, 1997

I remember Mark well! Mark was a good pilot, a quick learner, and had that special knack of doing the right thing in difficult situations. He was eager, he was smart and he was a good man. Always willing to do the most difficult task. Be proud—your brother was a brave man. Susan, you are now and always will be one of us—a Pink Panther.

I have always been proud of you, but more now than ever—having learned what you really did in Vietnam. I thought I knew, but I didn't. I always thought you were a good pilot. I just didn't know how good.

These emails from all over the country have touched my heart in a way I never expected. I guess that's why I held onto them for all these years. I am embarrassed to tell you how I thought our family were the only ones that went to The Wall and touched your name. I just had no idea. These guys never forgot you. And now decades later they have included me in their future! I am now a Pink Panther—in your place.

The truth is no one could ever take your place.

Love, Susie

WHAT IF?

Dear Mark,

June 21,1997, I received an email from Panther 21, Mike Jimison. He's still a helicopter pilot since his Army days. He's been flying to the off shore oil rigs the last twenty-four years. For the last eight years he's been working in Angola, West Africa. Ironically, this email came exactly twenty-eight years to the day, since that first telegram came telling us you were missing in action.

This is what he wrote me:

... I don't tell many war stories because if you tell one you have to listen to one and after twenty eight years I think I've heard them all. A handful of people know this story strictly for that reason.

In May of '69, I was assigned to the 361ˢᵗ ACE in Pleiku, Vietnam. When I arrived I was the only commissioned officer with three Warrant Officers like Mark. I was immediately assigned to the 2ⁿᵈ platoon, given a check ride in the aircraft and checked out in the area of operations. The present platoon leader was getting ready to rotate back to the States and I was slated to fill his position. I flew with Mark on many occasions but because of the hectic schedule, the first few weeks were a blur. I remember Mark as a dedicated and reliable pilot who was quiet and serious in a crowd of loud and rowdy pilots. I admit that I held up my end in that department. I don't re-member Mark ever involved in that; but like I said, the first few weeks were a blur.

I was assigned to do the scheduling in the platoon, which amounted to who would fly with who and when. Due to ex-

treme heavy activity at the time in our area of operations, everyone wanted to fly and every aircraft was committed. Six weeks passed and I had flown every day. The last Warrant Officers that arrived in country with me never got in-country check-rides because no aircraft was available. Assigned to labor details, like building revetments and repairing aircraft parking areas. We all wanted to fly because of all the action. Around the end of the sixth week and at the end of a very busy day, the new Warrant Officer that had arrived in-country with me declared he had finally gotten his check-ride and was cleared to fly. I told him that the schedule was up for tomorrow, but I promised to get him in the air the following day. He pleaded with me all the way to the officer's club where he was drowned out by loud music, drinking and the normal raucous behavior.

The next morning he showed up again in operations when we arrived to fly. I explained to him that everyone wanted to fly and nobody wanted the day off. Once again, he explained that for six weeks he had done nothing but hard manual labor and asked me again to fly, I reluctantly agreed to let him take my seat, because I hadn't had a day off in six weeks and a trip to the P.X. would be nice. I had to lend him my flight suit to wear because he hadn't received one yet.

I told him he would be flying with Mark and that he would see lots of action. His name was Mike Mahowald and he was killed with Mark that afternoon on his first operational flight. I'm not sure how it happened, but I think the scheduling board had never been changed and I was listed as M.I.A. with Mark.

It will be twenty-eight years next month and I still wonder what happened that day. The fact that it came real close to being me. It really didn't affect me until years later when I grew up a little and realized I wasn't bullet proof.

I haven't told many people this story like I said, but I am glad a member of Mark's family knows it and maybe someday Mike's family will too....

I was stunned. This man would not be alive had he flown that mission as scheduled June 16, 1969.

I lost touch with Mike for over two years after that email. Then on January 15, 1999, Pink Panther Jim Williams in California, instant messaged me on the computer and said he had someone online who wanted to talk to me. It was Mike Jimison—Panther 21, from West Africa.

We typed back and forth for about forty-five minutes and then Mike asked if he could call on the phone instead. We talked about the reunions I had been to in the past two years and I learned the reason he seemingly had dropped off the planet. He had come back to the States, diagnosed with a benign brain tumor, had it removed and was recuperating in Florida. We also talked about his first email and the events that led up to him giving up his seat June 16, 1969. He talked about the what if's—what if he had been flying with Mark; what if Mark had been shot, sitting in the back, and he had been in the front instead of Mahowald; with his experience, maybe the outcome might have been different.

Of course, we will never know the answers to those questions.

We talked on the phone every day. I learned about his kids, how he ran with the bulls in Spain, how his career has taken him all over the world since 1968, how he was grounded because of his brain surgery, and that his divorce was almost final.

I enjoyed Mike's sense of humor and our conversations. I very much looked forward to his phone calls. But I was newly divorced and NOT looking to add a man in my life, much less one that was 2500 miles away. I was a single Mom, raising an eleven-year-old son.

You know what they say about the best laid plans!

We talked every day for the next one-hundred-forty days, until we finally met face to face in Tennessee for the Vietnam Helicopter Pilots Reunion. Mike drove from Pensacola, I flew to Nashville, where Mike met me at the airport.

You would have thought at our age we wouldn't shake like a leaf during that first hug at the airport. We both did—a moment to remember!

It was the first reunion Mike had been to in several years. But it seemed like every time we got in an elevator or walked down the street, Mike ran in to someone he knew. I asked him how that could be when he never went to reunions!

"Flying for the largest commercial helicopter company in the world for over half your life, you meet a lot of other helicopter pilots. We were a dime a dozen after Vietnam. The Army trained thousands of us, and after Vietnam we were all looking for flying jobs; Petroleum Helicopters hired thousands of us."

After the reunion we talked at least once every day on the phone, and flew cross-country trips until July 2000 when Mike packed his truck and made the final cross-country trip from Pensacola to the State of Washington, where I had been living since 1995.

As serious as our relationship had become, I wanted to make sure before it became permanent that there was no confusion with loving me and survivor's guilt. So we took our time and made sure we married for all the right reasons.

On June 29, 2006, exactly seven years to the day we met in Nashville, we were married in a ceremony performed by a Vietnam Helicopter Pilot and Methodist minister, John Plummer. Then we spent our "honeymoon" at the Vietnam Helicopter Pilots Reunion!

During that reunion we took tour buses from the hotel to the Mall in Washington, D.C. It was the first time I had visited The Wall in D.C. with Mike and the rest of the Pink Panthers—also Bikini 29, Kent Harper. That feeling I had the first time in 1997 when I realized there were others who had not forgotten you, came rushing back. A feeling of relief and gratefulness.

I stood in the grass looking at the men I had met since '97, and remembered all those years of running my finger tips over your name on panel 22 West—thinking no one but your family ever did that. Smiling, I felt comfort on that sacred ground, just yards from your name.

The guys you spent your last nine months on earth with were there with me, including the wonderful man I had just married. Who could have known when I posted that first request online in 1997, searching for your Army unit in Vietnam, that my life would be where it is today. I feel so blessed!

That evening, back in the Panther Hospitality Suite, the Pink Panthers raised their glass in a toast to you and the other unit members lost, back in the day when they were young and bullet proof.

I did too.

Gone but not forgotten—I really know what that means now, Susie

It doesn't take a hero to order men into battle. It takes a hero to be one of those men that goes into battle.

—Norman Schwarzkopf

COUSIN JOHN, A FLYING TIGER

Dear Mark,

Aunt Arlene called yesterday and asked if I could stop by after work, she said she had something for me. She and Uncle Coston live only five minutes from me, so I go a few times a week whether I need to or not! Since Daddy has been gone ten years, and Mother lives on the East coast with Redina, Arlene and Coston are more like parents to me now than an aunt and uncle.

They still live on the same street where they were in 1968 when you had your layover on your way to Vietnam. Coston said he's always been thankful he drove the hour south to Fort Lewis and brought you to his house for a visit before you departed. The whole family enjoyed seeing you and remembers that week well.

After Daddy's and Coston's mother died in 1983, Coston ended up with her scrapbook. It was filled with letters, cards, announcements, and pictures. When he and Arlene returned from his mom's funeral in California, they put the scrapbook in a trunk.

During my visit last night, they wanted to give me the cards Daddy had sent his mother during the 1940s, when he was in the military. One Mother's Day card had a puffy center where he had attached tiny bomber wings. Much smaller than the miniature aviator wings you gave Mother. He had sent her birthday cards, a telegram announcing Linda's birth, and letters. I carefully removed the items from the scrapbook pages. Everything is over sixty years old now—all precious keepsakes.

I will give Linda the telegram announcing her birth. I know she will like that.

All four of Mom's sons had written letters home. Reading through the letters it was clear how much they loved their mother. During the war she must have looked forward to the mail every day.

Mom had pasted a newspaper article about the four Clotfelters serving in the military. Isn't it weird how we called both our grandmother's "Mom?" That must be why we ended up calling our mother, Mother, instead of Mom! So confusing!

Coston reminded me she had not one, but four "stars" in the front window of her home during World War II. It signified she had four from her family serving in the military. The stars were proudly displayed in windows back then. It wasn't the same during the Vietnam War, so often referred to as the unpopular war. I don't remember ever seeing a blue star in any window. We didn't even have one. Maybe Daddy thought it would cause retribution.

I pulled a folded-up piece of notebook paper out of an envelope that was glued to a page. Imagine my shock when I began reading this:

Dear Folks,

You must not feel badly about my death. The small part that I have played in the war, though it cost me my life, I am glad to give. Life has meant much to me, but not so much that I am too distressed at leaving and neither must you be. I had only a few things planned for the future. One of the most important was a nice home. Momma will please me very much if she will live in a more comfortable home with many flowers and trees. I am happy and so must she be.

Love, John

My first reaction was—who would write a letter like this? My second reaction—how would Mother and Daddy have reacted if you had written something like that?

I was so stunned I looked up to Coston for an explanation. He told me it was written by his first cousin—so our second cousin—in 1942. John Donovan was our Aunt Stella's older son. You remember Grandma's sister? She's been gone over twenty years now, too. John, a Flying Tiger, was shot down and Killed In Action while bombing the Hanoi airfield in Vietnam. The Japanese planes were being staged there during World War II. It was not yet Vietnam in 1942, it was still French-Indo China. While he was explaining, my thoughts were stuck on "you must not feel badly about my death."

I couldn't help but think about how the letter and losing John must have broken Stella's heart, but I also admired how thoughtful John was—trying to ease his mother's pain—even in death.

Coston went upstairs to make a copy of the letter for me. I sat there wondering if it was a premonition or just reality that he might not make it back that prompted John to write such a letter? When he returned with the copy, he brought down a book that had been his mother's. Her name was written inside. The book is called Chennault of the Flying Tigers, by Sam Mims, written in 1943. In Chapter 15 "Through the Eyes of a Tiger" there are thirty pages of excerpts of many of John's letters home. Coston let me borrow the book.

I kept going through the rest of the scrapbook even though I was distracted by John's letter. Imagine how surprised I was to see your handwriting towards the last few pages. I recognized your stationery, too. I pulled out the letter and found Mom had put a post card in the envelope, too. Your letter was in response to a letter you had received from her in October 1968. The letter was sweet and seemed like you didn't want to alarm Mom with the danger you had encountered. Your postcard made me smile. I'm in with a lot of real good officers and I'm flying the aircraft that I wanted to fly. I smiled because I have met these men and I know how much you liked the Cobra! Turning the page, I found an envelope from Daddy to his Mother with the newspaper article about your death. No letter, not sure there ever was one in the envelope.

Driving home I was still stunned, but also curious to learn more about John and the Flying Tigers.

I looked at a map of Vietnam on the computer when I got home and saw you were shot down only 1000 kilometers from where John was shot down. I couldn't help but think of the similarities between you two: both pilots, both single, both in wars to help other people. I realized how rich our family's military history is, but also sad for our tremendous sacrifice.

I wish you had known about John. He would have been your hero! I know you would have been fascinated in how he resigned his Navy commission to be a mercenary and help the Chinese fight the Japanese. He was promised his rank would be reinstated when he returned from China. That would never happen these days!

There are so many books written about the Flying Tigers and John is mentioned in most of them. However, I dug around enough on a Navy museum website and found thirty-nine pages of incredible letters he wrote home—all typed and single spaced! His brother Jim donated John's letters to a Naval Museum for preservation. I have some of your letters but not nearly that many.

I thought it was unusual you had a typewriter in a war zone, then I found out—John had one, too!

Anyway, John knew he would be more valuable to the Navy with combat experience and that was a big reason he became a mercenary. I think the money was a factor, also. 1941 wasn't long after the Great Depression. The American Volunteer Group, the Flying Tigers real name, were paid a handsome monthly salary ranging from $250-$750 depending on their job… from mechanics to squadron leaders. But that wasn't all. They were also promised a $500 bounty for every Japanese airplane they shot down. That sure was a lot of money in 1941!

But the money was only paid if they shot it down. Just damaging the plane didn't count. John was credited with shooting down four, which made him one short of being a flying ACE. You know how prestigious it was to be an ACE in those days! May 12, 1942, John was killed when his plane was shot down. I learned from a newspaper article, written in October 1942, that a Frenchman, Captain Pierre Pouyade, escaped from his Japanese captors in a fourteen-year-old airplane. He reported John had been buried in a ditch without military honors. Reading that bothered me—buried in a ditch. But then the Captain reported during that night, John's grave was covered in flowers three-feet high by French women. Knowing that must have been of some comfort to Aunt Stella. I wish there had been more in that newspaper clipping about John but there wasn't.

Aunt Stella was persistent in her plea to the French Embassy and high officials in Washington, D.C. before and after the war ended to bring John home. I called the cemetery and learned John was interred March 19, 1949 in his hometown of Montgomery, Alabama.

There have been many times I felt our family was one of the lucky ones. You were brought home. Yeah, you were classified missing, but for only a few weeks. Stella waited for seven years to get John home. Many families are still waiting. I think the unknown is worse. If there could possibly be a worse…

Love, Susie

As long as we live, they too will live;
For they are now a part of us, as we remember them.
—Rabbi Sylvan Kamens

IS IT A MEMORY OR A PHOTOGRAPH?

Dear Mark,

Sometimes I wish I could recall whole days and events with you, but I just can't. I see you sitting in a chair reading the funny papers on Sunday mornings. I see you sitting in your red MG in the driveway at the house on 60th Street in Hialeah. I can see you standing tall in your Army uniform at the annual electrician's picnic when you were home on leave. You looked so handsome.

But conversations and whole events just aren't that easily reconstructed, no matter how hard I try. Is everyone like that? I want to picture you in my mind, but sometimes I think I'm actually confusing a memory with a photograph. So I drag out pictures with hope it will jog my memory. Sadly, it never does.

I wonder if a lot of the reminiscences I used to have are now replaced by faded telegrams, a flag-draped casket, and my life without you. Does that mean bad memories outweigh the good? Does the bad push out the good? I'm not a brain or memory expert but I think that might be why I can't remember stuff—simple stuff, like sitting at the dinner table together.

I remember it was a round table—but I can't remember you sitting at the table. I remember Dan Rather and Walter Cronkite on the six o'clock news every night when we were at the table—showing us the war. After you were gone, it made me not want to eat.

I can't remember the day you left for Vietnam. But I remember the day we learned you would never come home.

I remember your personal belongings coming back. But I don't remember what happened to anything.

I want to remember your smile, your laugh, your walk. It hurts that I don't. I just didn't pay enough attention. Being too young, I didn't realize they were precious moments that I might never get back. Seems we took too much for granted.

So these letters to you will someday be how my grandchildren, and their children, will learn about their Great-Uncle Mark. And when I am gone, I hope they will still visit the Wall in D.C., and take their own children to honor your legacy and to keep your part of our family history from being lost through time.

I want them to be as proud of you as I am.

Love, Susie

But two minutes I will bide.
It's a pittance of time,
For the boys and the girls who went over.
In peace may they rest.
May we never forget why they died.
It's a pittance of time.

—Terry Kelly

THE WALL

Dear Mark,

The Vietnam Veterans Memorial in Washington, D.C., was dedicated Veterans Day, November 11, 1982. Most people remember the first time they saw The Wall. Whether it was in D.C. or the Traveling Wall. Whether it was last year or thirty years ago.

The half-scale replica was coming to Fort Lauderdale October 10, 1984. I had not seen the black granite monument in D.C. yet, so I felt compelled to go. I had only seen it on television, in the newspaper, and in magazines.

I needed to go.

It was evening, and we were inside a very warm, large, metal building in Port Everglades, in Fort Lauderdale. It had been fifteen years since we lost you. And even though I had never seen this wall or your name on a headstone, I didn't cry. Maybe I was following Mother and Daddy's cue—holding on to my emotions. There were thousands of people in that warm building, and so many were crying. Paul, my stepson, was old enough to drive there himself—and old enough to understand the expression of grief he was witnessing. He only stayed with us for a while. Little sister Heather, only six, already seemed worried about some of the people crying, so I held it together—as long as I could—until on the way home.

Silently, riding in the front seat, while my first husband, Kurt, drove home, I wiped tears away as secretly as I could. It was dark in the car, so that part was easy. Music on the radio was a good diversion for Heather—she sang along with Dolly Parton and Kenny Rogers, *Islands in the Stream*. For me too, as I drifted off in thought, wondering where fifteen years had gone.

You had been gone so long. I wondered if I would ever not miss you.

Some things never change. Every time I saw a photo of The Wall, I immediately search for your name. So, when a thirteen-part PBS documentary was playing on TV with footage of Vietnam, I sat down to watch it with hopes I could catch a glimpse of you or a Cobra. Instead, I heard it was a fool's war, the only war our country ever lost, one out of ten died, and showed piles of dead bodies. It was called Vietnam: A Television History. I felt as though someone had stabbed me in the chest.

I was home alone, and I cried for hours. It was like you had died all over again.

Not long after—weeks maybe—there was national attention to that documentary. A group called Accuracy in Media with Charlton Heston as its spokesman, countered with their own documentary, exposing the PBS lies and distortion. They also targeted CBS and the lies they had reported from the war zone, mainly by Dan Rather. They were demanding the truth on the very lies that had stabbed me in the heart. For me, it was too late, the damage had been done.

How could CBS and PBS be so insensitive to the living, and so dishonorable to the dead?

I remember the weekend when I watched that documentary more than I remember the first time I saw your name etched on the Wall in Port Everglades.

It took me years to really understand the war in Vietnam. But not quite so long to see through the media's slant .

No matter how long it took me to fully understand Vietnam, I never lost my pride in your service. I know you saved many American lives. You have always been my hero. And you still are.

Love, Susie

Other things may change us, but we start and end with family.

—Anthony Brandt

NOVEMBER 2012

Dear Mark,

Linda and I are driving to Maryland to visit Mother next month. Redina and Mike, their girls, and Nida will be there, too. We'll celebrate Mother's 90th birthday. Can you believe it? She is a tiny, frail, old woman now. Seems her only outing anymore is the occasional trip to the doctor. Her world has shrunk, yet she seems at peace with her life. I know you would appreciate all the effort and sacrifices Mike and Redina have made to keep Mother in their home and out of a nursing facility. Through all the operations, hospitalizations, and rehabilitations, Redina has navigated it all with her. I know if you were here you would have done your part. Redina takes care of her much like Mother's sister Millie took care of their mother in the 70s.

And we'll have birthday pie. Remember how Mother always preferred pie over cake? You only have one 90th birthday so she gets whatever she wants!

It is also the 30th anniversary of the Vietnam Veterans Memorial, in Washington, D.C., upon which your name is etched. I have the honor of reading your name again, like I did five years ago. Volunteers will read each name aloud—over 58,200 names—spanning four days. I am scheduled to read your name, Michael Mahowald's, plus twenty-eight others.

And as I always do, I will leave the words to the song Brother of Mine with your picture, laminated, at the base of your panel.

Mother's 90th birthday and the 30th anniversary of the Vietnam Veteran's Memorial—and forty-three years since you died. Seems like everything has changed in the world. Nothing is like it was when you left us in 1969. Yeah, we grew up, grew older, and grew wider!

Our family is spread out all over the country now. And with all the new technology, we can stay in touch effortlessly, not like the reel-to-reel tapes and slides you sent home from Vietnam. That was great for the times. You were ten-thousand miles away and, with those recorded tapes, we could hear your voice narrating as we saw each slide. Like you were right there with us.

Oh my gosh, now, though, you would be so amazed!

I wish you could see the dashboards in today's new cars with their audible directions and maps on a touch screen to guide you to your destination. Stereos and subwoofers—in cars! Cellular phones you talk into without using your hands! And in our homes, computers with screens—like live television, folks can see us and we can see them in real time.

Incredible changes have taken place the last forty-three years.

One thing never changed: I still miss you. When I am white-haired and ninety years old, I'll still remember—and still have you in my heart.

And I hope I will have succeeded in preserving your life story for future generations by writing about your twenty-two years on this earth.

I wish you hadn't missed all this fancy technology, because I know you would have loved it. But even more, I wish we hadn't missed the last forty-three years of your life. You would be sixty-five this year, and maybe have some white hair of your own. I can picture you behind the wheel of some fast red sporty car. And you are forever twenty-two.

You are always in my heart,
Susie

PHOTOGRAPHS

Gary Higgins and Mark after limping back to base.
"Nine Lives" chapter

Mother pinning Mark's wings on him at Fort Rucker, 1968.

Sherry and Mark, March 1968, in Texas.

Mark

Mark, Susan, Nida and Redina in Florida. September, 1964.

Christmas Card purchased on Fort Wolters Base, 1967.
This is where Mark got the idea to customize his van.

Mark and Daddy beginning the restoration on an MG in our backyard.
Hialeah, Florida, 1965

Orlando, Florida, July 1997. Meeting Gary Higgins the first time.

Linda, Art Cline and Susan.
Gary Higgins is holding the red notebook he had in Vietnam.

UNDER THESE ROTOR BLADES
PASSED THE FINEST HELICOPTER
STUDENTS IN THE WORLD
JULY 1, 1956 - AUGUST 16, 1973

Bob Garthwaite, Tom Grant and Susan in front of the Rotor blades
still at the Holiday Inn, 1998.

IN MEMORY: On Memorial Day, U.S. Rep. Jay Inslee delivered the Gold Star medal to Susan Clotfelter Blaker in honor of her brother, Mark Clotfelter, whose helicopter was shot down in Vietnam in 1969.

North Kitsap Herald newspaper article. Susan with now Governor of Washington State, Jay Inslee.

Julie and Susan at the Wall in Washington, D.C., Veterans Day.

Offerings at The Wall, Panel 22 West.

Packing the plane for our trip home from Omaha.
Daddy, Mike and Redina

Mr. and Mrs. Millard T. Clotfelter

request the honour of your presence

at the marriage of their daughter

Redina Diane

to

Mr. Michael E. Miller, Jr.

Saturday, the twenty-first of June

Nineteen hundred and sixty-nine

at ten o'clock in the morning

First Presbyterian Church of Hialeah

480 East Eighth Street

Hialeah, Florida

Reception

following the ceremony

660 East 60th Street

Hialeah, Florida

Redina and Mike's wedding day and the day we received the Missing In Action telegram. June 21, 1969

WESTERN UNION
TELEGRAM

CLASS OF SERVICE		SYMBOLS
This is a fast message unless its deferred character is indicated by the proper symbol.		DL = Day Letter
		NL = Night Letter
		LT = International Letter Telegram

The filing time shown in the date line on domestic telegrams is LOCAL TIME at point of origin. Time of receipt is LOCAL TIME at point of destination

```
501P EDT JUN 21 69 AA087
AA A WA136 JV XV GOVT PDB 10 EXTRA FAX WASHINGTON DC 21
203P EDT
MR AND MRS MILLARD T CLOTFELTER, DONT PHONE, CHECK DLY CHGS
ABOVE 75 CT, DONT DEL BTWN 10PM AND 6AM
    660 E 60TH STREET HIALEAH FLO
THE SECRETARY OF THE ARMY HAS ASKED ME TO EXPRESS HIS DEEP
REGRET THAT YOUR SON, WARRANT OFFICER MARK D. CLITFELTER HAS
BEEN REPORTED MISSING IN ACTION IN VIETNAM SINCE 16 JUNE 1969.
HE WAS LAST SEEN AS COMMANDER OF A MILIATRY AIRCRAFT ON A COMBAT
OPERATION WHEN THE AIRCRAFT WAS FIRED UPON BY A HOSTILE GROUND
FORCE, CRASHED AND BURNED. SEARCH IS IN PROGRESS AND YOU WILL
BE PROMPTLY ADVISED WHEN FURTHER INFORMATIONIS RECEIVED. IN
ORDER TO PROTECT ANY INFORMATION THAT MIGHT BE USED TO YOUR
SON'S DETRIMENT, YOUR COOPERATION IS REQUESTED IN MAKING PUBLIC
ONLY INFORMATION CONCERNING HIS NAME, RANK, SERVVICE NUMBER,
```
SF1201(R2-65)

WESTERN UNION
TELEGRAM

CLASS OF SERVICE		SYMBOLS
This is a fast message unless its deferred character is indicated by the proper symbol.		DL = Day Letter
		NL = Night Letter
		LT = International Letter Telegram

The filing time shown in the date line on domestic telegrams is LOCAL TIME at point of origin. Time of receipt is LOCAL TIME at point of destination

```
AND DATE OF BIRTH. THIS CONFIRMS PERSONAL NOTIFICATION MADE
BY A REPRESENTATIVE OF THE SECRETAY OF THE ARMY
    KENNETH G WICKHAM MAJOR GENERAL USA F 4 THE ADJUTANT GENERL
DEPARTMENT OF THE ARMY WASHINGTON DC
(430).
```

Mark at Camp Holloway

Mike and Susan were married June 29, 2006.
Officiated by John Plummer, Minister and Vietnam Helicopter Pilot

Mike and Susan celebrating their wedding weekend and
VHPA reunion. Washington D.C., 2006

Quintessential 1960s family

Julie and Susan, New Orleans, 2012

Photo courtesy of Norman Skipper

Paul Renner, Mark and Gary Higgins

Mark's graduation photo from Fort Rucker.

A Panther Cobra in flight. One of many aircraft Mark photographed.

Mark, Norman "Skip" Skipper and Harold Goldman

Mother, Redina, niece Lydia Miller and Susan at the Wall.
November 11, 1997

An ROTC representative from the University of Miami presenting
Mother and Daddy with Mark's posthumous medals. I am seated
behind my parents next to my niece, Denise.

Mark beside his VW van with helicopter caricature painted by friend
Lynn Wildman, 1967.

Sherry with Mark's VW van.

Emergency landing on Leghorn in "Nine Lives" chapter.
Photo Courtesy of Gladiator Ken Morrison

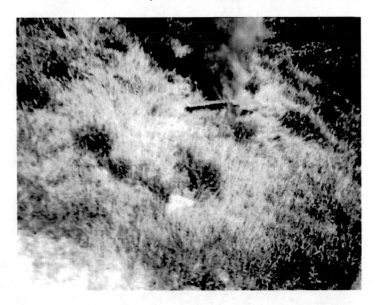

Cobra burning in elephant grass on December 1, 1968, following
strafing by Gary Higgins after Harold Goldman and Mark were rescued. Photo courtesy of Harold Goldman

Breakout tool from a Cobra—a gift from CW4 Frank Thoman.

30th Anniversary of the Vietnam Veterans Memorial with Julie Kink,
Washington, D.C.

WASHINGTON

23 July 1969

Dear Mr. and Mrs. Clotfelter:

It is with sadness that I write to you at this time of personal sorrow. The tragic passing of your son, Warrant Officer Mark D. Clotfelter, who was previously reported missing in Vietnam, is also a great loss to those who were privileged to serve with him in the United States Army.

I realize how difficult it must be to face the loss of a loved one and know that words alone offer little consolation. However, I hope that you will find some measure of comfort and gain inner strength in knowing how very important your son's selfless service was to his country.

The priceless gift of life is the most noble one a soldier can make to protect his loved ones at home and to safeguard the cherished beliefs for which his Nation stands. Our strength and security rest on the loyalty and devotion of American soldiers who today safeguard freedom as did American soldiers in earlier times of national peril. You can treasure the thought that for his gift of life your son is noble among men who share the blessings of freedom.

On behalf of all members of the United States Army, I express heartfelt sympathy.

Sincerely,

W. C. WESTMORELAND
General, United States Army
Chief of Staff

Mr. and Mrs. Millard T. Clotfelter
660 East 60th Street
Hialeah, Florida 33013

One of many letters sent to our parents.

Reading names during the 25th Anniversary commemoration of the Vietnam Veterans Memorial.

MARK D. CLOTFELTER, who graduated seventh in a class of 116 from the Army Aviation School at Ft. Rucker, Ala., became the 22nd Hialeah-Miami Springs youth to die in Vietnam.

Army Reports Missing Mark Clotfelter, Helicopter Pilot, Dead

The death of a 22-year-old Hialeah man, who was listed for a month as missing in action, has been confirmed by the U.S. Army.

Mark Clotfelter, a 1966 graduate of Hialeah High, was killed in Vietnam June 16 when his Cobra helicopter gunship came under heavy enemy fire. Clotfelter died when the helicopter plummeted to earth and burned in enemy-held territory near Dak To.

He was providing aerial support for a motorized reconnaissance convoy at the time.

It was more than a month before the Army could search the area to confirm the death. At least one other member of the crew was reported dead.

The young warrant officer was the son of Mr. and Mrs. Millard Clotfelter of 660 E. 60th St., Hialeah. A two-year veteran of the service, he had been in Vietnam nine months. He was the 22nd local boy to die in Vietnam.

Clotfelter, who served as a pilot gunner, was four times awarded the Air Medal. On Nov. 18 he participated in an operation that was credited with saving a troop carrier from total annihilation. He and others on the mission voluntarily drew the enemy fire from the besieged unit by placing themselves between the en-

was hit. When it crashed, he held down the advancing enemy with small arms fire. A third airship finally arrived and rescued the team.

In commending Clotfelter, his superior officers used such phrases as "courageous and dedicated," "great courage and devotion to duty."

According to the Army man's family, he was also slated to receive the Distinguished Flying Cross shortly before his death.

A graduate of Hialeah High, where he was a member of the chess club, Clotfelter attended Miami-Dade Junior College, taking courses in aviation. He wanted either to make a career of the service or to become a commercial pilot.

He received his pilot's license in June, 1967. Before enlistment, he worked for Aerodex and Chalk Airlines, and was employed part-time at John F. Kennedy Library.

At the Army Aviation School at Ft. Rucker, Ala., Clotfelter graduated seventh in a class of 116. He was stationed at Hunter AFB in Savannah, Ga., prior to his assignment in Vietnam.

Services were held Tuesday at Lowe-Hanks Funeral Home. Warrant officer Cl-

THE UNITED STATES OF AMERICA

TO ALL WHO SHALL SEE THESE PRESENTS, GREETING:

THIS IS TO CERTIFY THAT
THE PRESIDENT OF THE UNITED STATES OF AMERICA
AUTHORIZED BY ACT OF CONGRESS, JULY 2, 1926, HAS
AWARDED

THE DISTINGUISHED FLYING CROSS
FIRST OAK LEAF CLUSTER
TO

CHIEF WARRANT OFFICER (THEN WARRANT OFFICER) MARK D. CLOTFELTER, 267-78-1647, UNITED STATES ARMY

FOR HEROISM
WHILE PARTICIPATING IN AERIAL FLIGHT
IN VIETNAM ON 7 APRIL 1969
GIVEN UNDER MY HAND IN THE CITY OF WASHINGTON
THIS   22ND   DAY OF   SEPTEMBER   19 69

MAJOR GENERAL, USA
THE ADJUTANT GENERAL

SECRETARY OF THE ARMY

Camp Holloway, Pleiku, Vietnam II Corp

CWO Norman "Skip" Skipper, Lt. Paul Renner and
CWO Mark Clotfelter

Mark's legacy will live on in future generations.
Great-nieces August and Hazel Milleson visiting The Wall 2009
Photo courtesy of Heather Knapp

Chriss Cabodi, nephew and namesake of Chriss Roedinger, and Susan.
Veterans Day, 2012

Mark sitting on the Cobra's ammo bay doors.

> "Prairie Fire" are the words spoken when a cross border Special Forces team is compromised and running for the pick-up area. Your heart just stops when you hear those words. Your brother heard those words.
> —Mike Sloniker, LTC U.S. Army (Ret.)

NEW OLD LETTERS

Dear Mark,

Redina and Mike began some remodeling of their home for the first time in over twenty-five years. While we stood admiring the new colors on the walls, Redina told me that was not why she dragged me upstairs. She had found something she knew I would be very interested in! Cleaning out a storage area over the stairs, she had found two letters you had written her from Vietnam. I was thrilled! Redina then showed me some of her kids little booties, shoes and a pair of overalls she had made out of an old pair of jeans from the 70s. All the old things were pretty cool, but I couldn't wait to read your letters!

Finding a chair by the paint cans and stacks of new flooring, I read them in chronological order. In your letter from 1969 dated February 1st you asked Redina to send you a Ham Shack catalog. I never would have thought that you had time to talk on a Ham Radio while in a combat zone. But then, in another part of the letter, you talk about wanting to tape-record your missions. Maybe that Ham Radio catalog had the parts you needed for recording in the helicopter. A couple of your Army buddies mentioned how unique you were in your quest to record everything in-flight. Like the note I received from Bob Steen several years ago. He told me, "I remember tapes Mark made from a self-manufactured device consisting of a bundle of wires running from his helmet to a dilapidated battery powered recording device. He wanted the sounds of communications, rocket and mini-gun fire and the internal chattering between him and his fellow pilot. I used to tease him about his efforts in this regard and the seemingly difficult hassle it was to wire himself up prior to each and every time we launched!" I guess I am weird in not thinking anything of you doing all this wiring and recording. Sounds to me like something Daddy would have done!

Funny how you wrote differently to Redina, who is only four-and-a-half years older than me. I guess four years was a lot in teenage years when it came to comprehending war stuff. But then I never saw you write this kind of stuff to Mother—to not worry her.

> *...Last week my helicopter was hit with 50 cal. rounds and we came back streaming fuel. We were lucky it didn't catch fire. That was the first hit I've had in a month. Today was a day off but tomorrow we get to ride into battle again. I know Dad would like me to go into maintenance but I like flying into the hot areas too much right now.*

If I ever had any doubt that you loved what you were doing, this particular letter would put those doubts to rest. The truth is everyone knew you loved what you were doing. You were flying and saving American lives.

I have the picture you took of the Cobra that day. It's sitting in a huge puddle of fuel and quite a few guys standing around your very broken aircraft. They looked surprised you and Gary Higgins even made it back. Gary has told me about that day; but how cool is it—I can now read your version of what happened.

In this letter you thanked Redina for saying "hi" on the tape Daddy sent to you. I wasn't surprised that was all you got out of Redina. Seemed like we girls just froze back in those days every time we were put in front of a microphone and told to talk, whether it was Daddy's ham radio or the microphone on the tape recorder. It was second nature to Daddy. From World

War II radio communication—to the ham radio—to recording tapes to send you. I didn't know what to say to other amateur radio operators in countries on the other side of the globe, or even to you on those tapes. I was just better at writing letters.

I still have the newspaper article printed in The Miami New, about you being "On the Beam" when you were in elementary school. It told how much you liked talking on Daddy's ham radio to people all over the world. Mother was quoted in it saying how you were once a shy boy, but not any longer. The article boasts of how you increased your newspaper route, also. You were quoted in the article saying you wanted to keep on serving your customers to the best of your ability—the same way you served your country years later.

The date is not on the old news article but I am guessing it was about 1959, when you were in the sixth grade. You looked a little like Opie on the Andy Griffith Show. The picture shows an unconventional set-up of speakers and radios, probably similar to your unconventional set-up of wires and recording devices in the helicopter. Like father, like son!

The other letter Redina found is dated March 1, 1969. It was Redina's nineteenth birthday. You wrote that you were happy that Mike and Redina were planning on getting married. Of course you were—you are the one who introduced them! By letter or tape, you must have found out Mike had enlisted in the Air Force. I chuckled when I read:

...Let me know what he is doing in the Air Force. The Air Force people I've seen over here have it easy.

Mike didn't go to Vietnam. His expertise took him to Germany, where he was stationed twice, for a total of six years. Redina and Mike sure liked living in Germany and their first two children were born there.

The biggest surprise in this letter, though, was you telling Redina that you and Sherry had been discussing marriage for quite some time. I thought I had made that up in my hopelessly-romantic teenage mind. I loved how you said her family had been very nice to you, and that she was a good girl! You know I contacted her in 1997; I already wrote you that a few years ago. She was so sweet and seemed to really appreciate me getting in touch with her. Did my heart good to hear how she had not forgotten you! I always knew in my heart that you and Sherry would have been married had you returned from Vietnam. Now I wonder what happened to all the letters you two wrote to each other. Maybe someone will find them tucked away someday.

Today though, I am very thankful Mike and Redina are remodeling and they too, saved your stuff like I have.

Your sister, Susie

Brothers and sisters are as close as hands and feet.
—**Vietnamese Proverb**

THE FLORIDA ROOM

Dear Mark,

You never complained about living with all sisters. Or about not having your own bedroom. Or even about not having a bedroom at all. Your room was the Florida room, which was the only way to get to the back porch where the washer and dryer were. It sure lacked privacy. I don't remember much about the Florida room except it had French doors, windows, and that is where your snake was. And the iguana. And the Caiman alligator. So I didn't pass through there much. The safest route for me was out the front door and then around the house. It didn't matter what the menagerie were safely housed in—I still didn't want to be near any of it.

I don't remember you being home much during your high school days. You worked at JFK Library and Goodyear Tire, and when you weren't working, you were outside tinkering with one sports car or the other. I don't remember you ever hanging out in "your room." The record player was in the living room, so I did get to listen to your music. *Surfer Girl* and *The Little Old Lady from Pasadena* was much better than Mother's *Tumbling Tumble Weeds* and *Georgie Girl*.

Funny how I never forgot you didn't have a real bedroom. I guess it bothered me when I got older. It must have made sense at the time, because we only had three bedrooms. I wish things had been different.

Thank you for not making me feel bad that I had a bedroom, even if I was sharing it with Redina and Nida. Remember when Linda got married in 1962—and Redina got her room? Maybe you should have gotten Linda's old room. Redina, Nida and me in one room got a little crowded the older we got! You know, the bigger we got. But I think you probably should have been the one moving into Linda's old room.

Nida and I shared a room until Redina got married in 1969. That summer is a blur, but I know I moved in to Redina's room.

Finally, in Vietnam, you got your own room!

Norm Skipper, Al Porter and, I think, Bob McFall shared a hooch with you in Vietnam. The hooch was divided into four rooms. The rooms were on the corners of the building and had a common area in the middle. Al Porter told me you and he had the two rooms on the south side. "As you entered the door, take a left and enter Mark's room, and a right to enter my room. Mark was always in his room working his tape recorder and cleaning up—he was very neat. He spoke often of his family in Florida."

I'm sorry you never had a cool room of your own when you were growing up. And I am glad you finally got your own room—in the hooch.

Love, Susie

Most of the remains are taken from Dover
AFB by hearse to the airport in Philadelphia
for air transport to their final destination.
When the remains of a service member are
loaded onto a hearse and ready to leave the
Dover mortuary, there is an announcement
made over the building's intercom system.
With the announcement, all service members
working at the mortuary, regardless of service
branch, stop working and form up along the
driveway to render a slow ceremonial salute
as the hearse departs.

—U.S. Marine Lt. Col Michael Strobl,
Taking Chance

IDPF

Dear Mark,

I know you've heard the expression, "Be careful what you
ask for." Well, it's sitting here next to my computer. It's called
the Individual Deceased Personal File. I'd never heard of it before until one night Julie and I were talking on the phone. She
told me she had requested David's IDPF to see what medical
care he was given immediately after his helicopter crashed, and
then later at the hospital in Japan where he eventually died.

The very next day I sent a written request for your IDPF.

There's another expression I now wish I'd also heeded: Some
stones are better left unturned.

The first time I opened the IDPF and saw renderings of
where your bones were burned and what parts were missing, I
shut the file and put it in a drawer—vowing to never open it
again. That was nearly thirteen years ago.

But last month I needed the exact co-ordinates of where
you were shot down. I know this sounds odd, but a former
Marine, Ed Gar, was going back to Vietnam soon and asked if
I knew exactly where your crash site was. I pulled the file from

the drawer thinking I would like to know what is there now. It could be overgrown brush. It could be a freeway. After I got what I needed for Ed I began to read some of the pages. That was something I just couldn't do when I first received this file over a decade ago.

Your name had been handwritten on the cover years ago but what startled me was a stamp, not handwritten: Best Copy Possible, Poor Quality Original. I was expecting the worst, but the entire document is legible.

Who knew the first page would be an itemized bill from Dover Air Force Base for their services?

Standard Casket $140.00
Transportation (Pick Up) $4.00
Other Services (Weighing) $.85

Was Daddy expected to pay for this? Or was it the government that received the bill? Whatever, this seemed an odd place for a bill. Who charges anyone .85 cents for weighing?

Government furnished items:
Transportation of Remains $99.69
Transportation Escort $101.00
Interment Expenses $500.00
Flag and flag case $6.40
Clothing, Decoration, Insignia $49.35

Clothing? What clothing? Your casket was closed, so I don't understand that item. Further into the document it clearly states you were "properly wrapped and secured in position." That doesn't sound like a uniform was needed.

Insignificant items like the foreign money you had, had to be converted to U.S. dollars, and a registered letter with the check was sent to Daddy. A whole page was dedicated to two dollars that was converted. Mike says you guys were paid in Military Payment Certificates, or MPC's, while in Vietnam, so it was no surprise you didn't have cash in your hooch.

Certificate of Destruction is an entire page dedicated to explaining seven slides that *The Summary Court* deemed *detrimental* to Next of Kin and were destroyed. Seriously, they could have just destroyed the slides they were referring to and no one in our family would ever have known. It wasn't important anyway.

Every time I run across a dollar amount it annoys me even more. Daddy was coping with enough without having to see the cost of this and the cost of that on so many telegrams. Shouldn't the military and the government take care of everything? After all, it's their fault for sending you into harm's way in the first place.

The next fifty-two pages is documentation after documentation of positive identification, copies of telegrams, the condition you were in and, finally, the escorting of your remains back to Daddy.

I noticed the name of the man assigned to escorting you from Dover to Miami International Airport and finally to Lowe-Hanks Funeral Home on Okeechobee Road in Hialeah. I can only imagine how difficult escorting someone back to a heartbroken family must be. It was Tuesday, July 29, 1969—I was fourteen. Until reading the escort's debriefing, I didn't know that Daddy had taken time off from work to meet you at the funeral home. I would have been there, too, but no one asked me to go. School was out for summer break. I wish I could remember what I was doing that day, but when I try to recall anything back in those days, the only thing that comes to mind is Mother lying in her bed with a wet washcloth on her forehead. She did that a lot back then.

I am grateful Mother and Daddy never read the government's words: not recognizable, mangled, severely burned and mutilated, non-viewable remains. Some things are better left unsaid.

Flipping pages, I see your name and evacuation number frequently. But I also see your face. It's a copy of your initial Armed Forces I.D.

You were so young.

I stare at it—seeing a little of Mother in your face and a little of Daddy. A few people have told me I resemble you, but it's hard for me to see. Especially now that I am nearing three times the age you were when I saw you the last time.

Record of Recovery: (When they finally got you out of the Cobra)
July 2, 1969
Evacuation Number 180/243/083
Map Sheet Number 6538 III.
YB 902274 ENE of Dak To
Approximately 30 meters North of Highway 512
In wreckage of Cobra Helicopter around area of pilot seat.
2 I.D. tags inside Nomex Flight Suit as follows
top CLOTFELTER, MARK D.
W3 161 105
Name tape on suit jacket CLOTFELTER.

Morticians Anthropologist Mortuary Decedent Routine. Words I never associated with you, but now I read them on every page, of every detailed identification procedure.

I wonder if you thought the X-rays the Army took of your teeth during basic training were probably not to check the health of your teeth as much as it was for positive identification later. I also wonder if those dental records were already in Vietnam, in case they were needed.

Your Certificate of Death (Overseas) says your death was a homicide by hostile fire. I don't think I ever thought of it as homicide. But now that I have read it, it makes sense.

The Field Search Record was filled out by the 243d Field Service Co (GR). It documents the recovery of you and Mike Mahowald on July 2, 1969—sixteen days after you were shot down.

Hidden on a darker gray paper marked unclassified (I almost missed) it says: Officially recommended for promotion

June 10, 1969. Eligible for promotion July 16, 1969. I hope you knew that.

I could have lived the rest of my life without the details in this file. Seeing how broken and burned you were hurts. But I also saw your death was "Immediate." Something I think we all knew but after reading it, all doubt is put to rest. The careful process of positively identifying our war dead is professional and respectful, and for that I am grateful.

They have left no doubt in my mind.

Since 1997, my only desire has been to learn how you lived your last nine months. I learned how you worked and how you played. But in the process, I also learned how you died and the meticulous process that followed.

No one else needs to see the IDPF. I have filed it away again. But maybe this document is better shredded. The original still remains with the Army—as it should.

Love you always, Susie

MEDALS

Dear Mark,

Over the years I've heard more than once that you guys didn't fly to earn medals. I've been told you flew for each other. It makes sense when I hear of guys like Kent Harper, Bikini 29, who flew into hell for people he didn't even know. Rescuing those under fire, injured and those who most likely would have died had he not gone in for the pick-up. Men like you, my Mike, and the entire Pink Panther unit who provided cover to allow these types of very dangerous pick-ups—under fire yourself! The end result being a safe evacuation of Americans you probably never knew or would ever see their face.

In your letter dated November 7, 1968 you told me that it made you feel good to get soldiers out of grave danger. Just in case you don't remember what you wrote I added your original letter here:

Dear Susie,

I am being careful. But I do get into some
good action. Like yesterday, we were called to
help three foot soldiers who were traped on top
of a hill in a foxhole with NVA coming up on all
sides. The army had artillery going into the
side of the hill but things were not looking very
good for the three in the hole.

I was in a light fire team of Cobras that came
to help with two UH-1 slicks. We shot up the hill
on all sides for about ten minutes then came in with
the slick aircraft to give it cover. The three ran
to the helicopter and thay came out. All this
time we were shooting rockets and guns to try
and keep the enemy from hitting the helicopter.

I am very sure, with out our gun cover,
thoes three men whould have been lost. This type
of mission makes us fell good because we did our
job, and did it well.

Please tell Mom not to send any food to me.
I'm able to get enough to eat and we try not to
have any food in our hoch because of a rat problem.
We don't have rats but other people do.

Your school grades arn't bad. You are getting
about the same in Math as I was in English, But you
can do better.

2

The typewriter I'm useing is an "Olivetti
Underwood" that I just got today. I'm not as
good with it as I used to be but I'll learn.
Some of my slides are coming back from
Kodak and I will send some with a tape soon.
This week I also got a slide viewer made by the
Argus co.
Let me know what Linda and Dennis are upto.
Mother should send in that order for Xmas soon.
To relax the Officers Club showes films and
has a live show on stage about twice a month.
Drinks are 30¢ and beer is 20¢.
I must go so just write if you can or even
better, send a tape.

Love,

101 Mark D. Clotfelter
361st. Avn. Co.(escort)
APO. 96318 SF

FREE

96318
NOV 10
1968

Miss. Susie D. Clotfelter
660 E. 60st.
Hialeah, Florida
33013

Your letter is clear about the mission—rescue the men or they will die. Also, you were right about my math grade. I could have done better! But after all these years, math is still not my strong suit.

Back to my point about the medals...

Mike once said something like those that talk the most about what they did in Vietnam, probably did the least.

Others have reiterated that very same sentiment to me. Lately in the news, too frequently, we're told stories of men shown in military uniforms. Their chests full of medals—medals they could never have earned if they had been in the military fifty years! It's hard for me to imagine why someone would want to lie about what they did while allegedly serving our country.

A book came out in 1998 that exposes fraudulent claims of extraordinary heroics earning extraordinary medals. *Stolen Valor* by B.G. Burkett and Glenna Whitley is the go-to book for the truth about Vietnam veteran wannabes. Who knew it would be so prevalent?

Are the wannabes those who never went to Vietnam? Are they the draft dodgers that burned their draft notice and ran away to Canada? Or are they so deficient of self-esteem they fabricated their past to concoct something they never were?

Stolen Valor, complete with photos, opened my eyes to the who's and why's of those claiming great heroics in a war most never saw. Jug Burkett called them fakers—I call them liars. Had you survived the war, I'm sure you would have this book on your shelf just as I do. The lies and false claims became so widespread that President George Bush signed into law The Stolen Valor Act in 2006. The law made it a misdemeanor to wear uniforms decorated with medals that were purchased — not earned. Unfortunately, in 2012, the U.S. Supreme Court deemed it "freedom of speech" to fabricate great heroic stories in military service.

I don't think the courts have heard the end of it yet!

Then there are the guys like Mike—yes, my Mike. You will never hear him speak about medals he earned during his tour in Vietnam. He just doesn't talk about it. If prodded, he might mention he has a Distinguished Flying Cross (DFC). But never would you hear he was awarded three. The documents are buried deep in a file cabinet. The embossed certificates that are suitable for framing, aren't.

What has been important to him—because it had a direct affect on his employment—are his flight-hours and his medical records. Dating back to flying the TH-55 at Fort Wolters to the end of his forty-three-year career flying helicopters, Mike's hours and medical history have always mattered. He says no employer ever cared about any DFC or Air Medals. Mike downplays medals, but never forgets certain days. Like the day we lost you. And the day his front-seater, Marvin Spieker, was shot in his femoral artery, blood gushing to the floor of the Cobra. And the day Michael O'Donnell, a Bikini pilot, was killed. Those memories remain, all too vivid—like it was yesterday.

Michael O'Donnell, flying a Huey, and my Mike, flying a Cobra, were among those involved in a mission to extract a Long Range Reconnaissance Team, RT Pennsylvania, that had been under fire all night. The Bikini creed is "You take them in, you get them out." Although it was a desperate situation, the LRRPs had to be rescued. O'Donnell risked his life—and lost it—to save men he didn't know. The Special Forces team was under fire and O'Donnell knew from his LRRP radio contact on the ground that the men had to be evacuated or they would die. Under fire, O'Donnell went into a hot LZ. Once everyone climbed aboard, his chopper began its ascent out of the canyon. About one hundred meters from the pick-up, his aircraft was hit by small arms fire and immediately exploded.

After a moment of disbelief, my Mike is quoted in several books and online web sites about the O'Donnell crash. Mike was the closest to the explosion and his voice was the first everyone heard on the radio: "I don't think a piece bigger than my head hit the ground." He's told me many times he wishes he hadn't said it that way, that he should have chosen better words. Who knew that one sentence would be echoed so many times?

It was a horrific moment.

No one can criticize that comment—they weren't there. Mike didn't high-tail it out of there, either. He made a pass into that Cambodian canyon, all the while under fire to see if there were survivors. Bikini Jim Lake also flew in looking for survivors. But the ground fire was so intense they had to leave. It was a hard day for the Bikinis and the Pink Panthers— returning to base without the Bikini crew and passengers.

CPT Michael O'Donnell—aviator, singer, guitar player and poet—had written a poem a month before he was KIA. It is so poignant, so appropriate, because we should never forget.

If you are able, save them a place inside of you

and save one backward glance when you are leaving for the places they can no longer go.

Be not ashamed to say you loved them, though you may or may not have always.

Take what they have left and what they have taught you with their dying and keep it with your own.

And in that time when men decide and feel safe to call the war insane, take one moment to embrace those gentle heroes you left behind.

Major Michael Davis O'Donnell 1 January 1970 Dak To, Vietnam

The entire crew and passengers on that fateful rescue attempt were finally recovered in 1998. The aircraft and its human remains were positively identified and eventually buried. In 2001, in a single casket at Arlington National Cemetery, the Bikini crew and the RT Pennsylvania Special Forces unit were paid final respects. I wish Mike and I had been able to attend.

My Mike seldom uses the word "hero." He thinks the word is drastically overused—and that its true meaning has been diminished because of it. But I think it is safe to say he would consider Michael O'Donnell a "gentle hero."

I know you would have been like Mike—and like Daddy was following World War ll. Proud to have helped other Americans—ones you never knew or saw. Never boastful. And also like Mike, remembering the significant days when all the heroics in the world couldn't prevent losses like you and Michael O'Donnell.

You always closed your letters by asking me to write again. Here I am, forty-four years later still writing you letters. Still missing you.

Before the medals—before you went to Vietnam—I had only thought you hung the moon. The difference now is…

I know you did.

Love, Susie

p.s. Even with all the typos, your letters to me are priceless!

No good decision was ever made in a swivel chair.
—U.S. Army General George S. Patton, Jr.

FIELD SEARCH

Dear Mark,

I dragged a couple of boxes out of the closet I'd stashed there in 2009, the year Mike and I first moved to Georgia. I was looking for my Hialeah High School yearbooks and ran across a small stack of letters with a rubber band around them, and a computer print-out of names. I remembered that stack well!

I told you before that Nida had brought me a list from her computer after I gave her three names I found in your paperwork and pictures.

The first was Paul Renner, whose name I found on paperwork for your Army Commendation Medal. I sent out about twenty letters—all the same—with a self-addressed stamped envelope, so they could answer me and not cost them anything other than a couple of moments of their time. I simply asked if they were "the same Paul Renner that served with my brother, Mark, in Vietnam," and I included, "if you aren't, it would help if you would please let me know, using the stamped envelope I've enclosed." I received fifteen back—all with sweet notes— but none the right Paul Renner.

...I am sorry but I am not the same Paul Renner. I was never in Vietnam. I wish you best of luck and hope you have success.

...I am writing for my husband. He was never in the war. I think what you are doing is a wonderful thing. We are very sorry we can't be of any help. Good luck in your search. We hope you find what you are looking for.

...I offer my condolences for the loss of your brother. I thank him for the ultimate gift he gave for our freedom and our country. The Paul Renner you addressed your letter to is my son and he said he already answered you. He now lives at another address. I am his mother. He, too, thanks your dear brother. Good luck to you.

Another name I sent letters to was Robert Rodgers. I wrote a different letter to him because he was your commanding officer when you first arrived in Vietnam. Again, I didn't find him, but heard back from such nice people.

...Sorry, I'm not the one. I was in the Army August 71 thru August 73 and was state-side the entire time. Good luck—I hope you find the person you are looking for.

...Wish I could be of help, but I am not the Robert Rodgers you are seeking. I retired from the military after World War II. I know it hurts to lose a brother. I hope you will be able to find more information. Should I ever run into the other Robert Rodgers, I'll keep your name to give to him. Good luck.

And the last person I tried to locate was Robert Furney, your second commanding officer. I found his name on the KIA notification letter from Vietnam. The responses were similar to what I received back from the Paul Renner's and Robert Rodgers, except for two.

...Sorry, but I can't help you. My middle initial is E. But more importantly, I didn't go to Vietnam because my brother was killed in a Navy dirigible accident in 1960 when he was 21 and I was 19. Best of luck in your search. I have never been one to look up people with the same name in other cities, so I can't help in that way either.

...I am not the Robert Furney you are looking for. Try this man, I get his mail sometimes...

I immediately sent a letter to the address he suggested. On April 28, 1997, I found out the suggested address was right. I received a four-page, single-spaced, typewritten letter back from Major Robert Furney, your commanding officer. He told me about the indigenous people of South Vietnam—the primitive Montagnards—who worked side by side with our Special Forces.

He also wrote of his idea to use two teams of two Cobras instead of one team of two that was being used when he first took over the unit. He felt it was safer and implemented it as procedure.

He told me that his mother had a friend whose son went missing during World War II. That poor mother held out hope for the rest of her life that her son would be knocking on her door any day. He didn't want that for our mother. He said he wrote the first letter to Mother and Daddy with that in mind. He didn't want to raise false hope, because he had an eyewitness who was sure no one could survive such a crash—your wingman, Alan Porter. But because the area was too dangerous to get a search-and-recovery team in—to get you and Mike Mahowald out—he could only report you missing.

When I first received the letter, I felt good about it. It was informative. Precise. In my letter to him I had only asked if he was the right Robert Furney. He must have assumed I wanted to know how you died. But it's been years now and I've received many letters about you and the day of your crash, and now I see his letter quite differently.

...Someone in the underground bunker at Dak To requested that a reconnaissance be made of the road from Dak To to Ben Het to get a feel for the level of entrenchment by the Viet Cong and to determine if it was feasible and or possible to run in a relief column as a ground convoy to the besieged

camp. For some reason, rather than passing the request over to the Air Cavalry unit as they should have done, my guys from the 361ˢᵗ said that they would do it. A can-do attitude. It was on this reconnaissance mission that his helicopter was hit and shot down.

What was very upsetting was that it was not our unit's type of mission, to conduct a reconnaissance. We were fire support. Reconnaissance was a perfect Air Cavalry Unit mission for that is what they were designed and equipped to do with scout helicopters, a few gunships, and some ground infantry troops carried in UH-1's. I was unable to get support for the ground recovery operation for several days and finally five of us just flew in and made the recovery. It was sad, hard and brought tears to my eyes. It was my goal to have all my guys come home alive. This was my second tour in Vietnam when I commanded the 361ˢᵗ. I briefed every incoming man—officer, warrant officer and enlisted—that I didn't want them to take any chances, don't stick your neck out, don't try to be a hero as you could see where the war was going—phasing down. I didn't want any heroics that might cost a life.

After sixteen years, I do read it differently. It kind of feels as if he is blaming you guys for accepting the mission. As your commanding officer, I guess he has that right. But you guys were the ones waiting in Dak To, ready to fly a mission like the Panthers did every day. And Furney was still back at Camp Holloway. You guys on duty—ready to launch on a moment's notice—were the ones who ventured into the fight every day. I can see you volunteering to take this mission. I think you went because you knew it was necessary to get the truck convoy up the road and you felt that you could help that happen.

Furney also wrote:

After we were able to get into the site, recover the bodies and obtain positive identification, I wrote and sent my second letter to your family reporting his untimely death.

I kind of doubted that Major Furney actually went to the crash site. Maybe it was just a figure of speech. It didn't sound right that a commanding officer would be so hands-on. Especially since I knew he didn't fly as much, not like the rest of you guys. So, I dragged out your Individual Deceased Personal File once again and flipped page-after-page until I got to the Field Search Record. Forty-two pages in, between the Dental Charts and Skeleton Charts. I found the name, grade, service number and organization of the man who actually recovered you and Mike Mahowald. His name is SGT Glynn Kohler. His organization, the 243d Field Service Co. (GR). That stands for Graves Registration, which did recovery, identifications procedures and preparations for all the KIA's during the war, prior to the remains being sent home. They were the mortuary people. His report: Place of Recovery: *From the Burned Aircraft's wreckage*

> *On 2 July 1969, this unit conducted a Search & Recovery mission involving a Cobra Helicopter that crashed near Dak To, RVN. The team arrived at the scene of the wreckage and made a thorough ground search of the area approximately 10 meters from the wreckage. This search was hampered by dense undergrowth. A search of the burned aircraft revealed portions of mangled remains. Portions of remains were removed from two (2) areas of the craft and kept segregated. A result of the area and wreckage was conducted 2 July 1969 with negative results.*

I thought about it a while, trying to ignore the word that hurt—mangled—and wondered if I could find Glynn Kohler. I didn't really think I would have much luck. But after typing his name into my computers search engine, I found his name associated with a mortuary license. That had to be him! His first name has a unique spelling and after his job in Vietnam, mortuary made sense. I searched further and came up with a phone number.

But now that I found him, what would I ask? I knew I didn't want to know what he saw in the Cobra.

Cold calls are the worst. Not just for me, but more for whoever is at the other end of the phone. I've done a few over the years and know email or letters are best. Even leaving a message on someone's phone is better than an unsuspecting person at the other end getting a call about something that happened over forty-years ago. It gives the person a chance to collect their thoughts and choose their words.

After introducing myself, I quickly told Glynn I would never be able to tell anyone what I was doing that many years ago, so, if he didn't remember, I would understand.

Imagine my surprise when Glynn said he did remember that day, for a couple of reasons. One, because there was a Major right there at the crash site. He assured me that was rare. For that reason alone it stood out in his mind. Glynn reflected on the helicopter ride out, saying he didn't remember what unit took him into the crash site, but did remember the pilot and crew were in a subdued mood. This was the case in most of the recoveries. The mood on the return flight was as somber as on the ride in.

A moment he never forgot was when "the Major helped me load the two body bags into the aircraft when it was time to leave."

I was so wrong.

Furney saying he was able to get into the site was not a figure of speech.

The next time I see Bob Furney, I'll look at him differently. With more respect. He didn't have to be there or do that.

Then, the next thing Glynn told me gave me goose bumps!

He said there was something else different about this recovery—One of the pilots was wearing someone else's clothes. That just about took my breath away. He said it was the only time that had ever happened on all recoveries he was involved in. I told him he was only the second person ever to tell me that story—the other was my husband. I then told him a little of the story about how Mike Jimison was supposed to be flying with you that day and Mike Mahowald was wearing Jimison's Nomex. Not that I ever doubted Jimison's story, but hearing it from Glynn just made it more real. It left no doubt in my mind he truly remembered that day.

Wow, this turned out to be a long one. In retrospect, I know now that trying to find your unit was not real successful by mailing out random letters to people. I did find Major Furney that way, though. I guess I can throw out all those letters now. I'll keep Major Furney's.

Tonight, I'll say a special prayer for Glynn Kohler and Major Furney—they got you home. I think of all the parents and siblings that are still wondering about their loved one who never came home from a war. I know I've said it before ...it was terrible that we lost you, but the not knowing would have been worse.

Love, Susie

BREAK-OUT KNIFE

Dear Mark,

I should have told you this in the last letter, because it concerns Glynn Kohler. I have to tell you what happened the day he called. Be it a coincidence or chance. Fate or destiny. Whatever it is, I believe it is something.

Actually, Glynn was returning my call. I had called him earlier and he was in the middle of helping his wife, who had broken her shoulder recently, get out of the tub. So he said he would call me back shortly. Before he hung up, he asked, "What was your brother's name so I can refresh my memory?" I told him, then we hung up.

Soon, I heard the doorbell. It was the mailman, dropping a box on the front porch. He was hopping back into his mail truck by the time I opened the front door. I carried my cell phone with me—I didn't want to miss Glynn's call. Picking up the box, I noticed on the return label it was from Frank Thoman.

Frank is a Dustoff pilot, you know—a military air-ambulance—and we have a mutual friend, Hank Cramer. Frank had done a tour in Afghanistan, in support of Operation Enduring Freedom, but is back in the States now. I haven't actually met Frank yet, except through Facebook. In 2011, we sent books to his unit when they were deployed.

On September 11, that same year, his unit flew a full-size American flag on their Blackhawk helicopter and then sent us the flag and a certificate in appreciation of us for thinking of them.

The top of the certificate has an American flag on the left corner and the black, green and red Afghan flag on the right.

In beautiful color, there's a map of Afghanistan—superimposed with a Blackhawk flying a flag. The certificate says the accompanying flag was flown by F CO 1-126th Unit on a UH-60 Tail # 79-23327, it symbolized the sovereign power of the United States unshakable resolve to keep our country safe.

You would like the motto on their unit patch: In Chaos There is Hope. Nicknamed Chaos Dustoff!

Frank knows about you and that you were a helicopter pilot. He's marveled about all you had done in your short life. Last week he asked for my address because he had something he wanted to send me. I'd forgotten I'd sent it until I saw the return address with his name on this package.

I had the box, a knife I'd retrieved from the kitchen, and my cell phone in my hands, so I sat on the front porch swing and cut the tape on the box. I pulled out a note Frank had left on top of the bubble wrap. In his note he said that he *pulled this knife out of an AH-1F Cobra helicopter in 2000. The knife was used as a back-up system for a Cobra in case your plastic canopy failed to open in an emergency. You would score the plastic with it, then punch the window and break out of the aircraft. They refer to it as the break-out knife. I hope you don't mind, but I thought you should own it.*

I pulled out all the wrapping and began unrolling it to find the 7 ½ inch-knife (which looks more like a heavy tool)—and then my phone rang. It was Glynn Kohler.

I have to stop right here to say: What are the chances of me holding my phone in one hand talking with the man who physically removed you from the wreckage, and in the other hand was a Cobra break-out knife that could have provided an escape for you had that crash not been as awful as it was.

Coincidence? Seems like something more than that to me.

Whatever it is, you are still touching lives—especially mine.

Love, Susie

The road is long
With many a winding turn
That leads us to who knows where
Who knows where
But I'm strong
Strong enough to carry him
He ain't heavy, he's my brother
—The Hollies
(B. Scott - B. Russell)

GREEN BERET

Dear Mark,

This might sound a little crazy, but I think someday I would like to share these letters with those who have experienced a similar loss. If someone can learn from our family's tragedy, then the sharing will be worth it.

There's a war going on in Afghanistan. The war in Iraq, which has lasted more than seven years now, is drawing to a close. Most of the troops have come home. Thankfully there are less and less of our military being killed.

I remember the day I heard that SGT Nathan Chapman, from Fort Lewis, had been killed in Afghanistan. It was January 4, 2002. My first thought was *here we go again.* He was a young Special Forces officer, with a wife and two small children. I followed his story from the announcement of his death to his burial at Tahoma National Cemetery. I thought about him a lot, wondering if he had a sister or a brother. The newspapers, as usual, focused on the tragedy of his death. They featured a heart-wrenching photo of his twelve-month-old son, wearing a miniature version of his father's green Class A dress uniform. It was just like his Daddy's—three chevrons and two rockers, denoting a sergeant first class. His widow, Renae, dressed in black, stood beside him, holding the toddler's favorite blanket.

Daughter Amanda was smelling flowers nearby. I thought of the long road ahead of them.

In an article about his memorial service being held at the 1st Special Forces headquarters on base, the newspaper article mentioned my friend Hank Cramer was in attendance. He came to honor the first Special Forces officer killed, like his own father had been forty-five years earlier in the Vietnam War. But that's not where the similarities end. Like CPT Cramer, they were both second-generation military, both dedicated members of the 1st Special Forces, and both doting husbands with young families.

Nathan Chapman and his family have remained in my thoughts and prayers, even though it has been over ten years now. I saved the newspaper clippings. I look at the two children in the picture, hoping Brandon and Amanda have adjusted to their Daddy never coming home. Then I think about Hank Cramer and the adjustments he had to make.

Could my book even help Brandon and Amanda?

There was live coverage of SGT Chapman's funeral. President Bush spoke of the loss in a televised conference, and the local newspaper coverage was abundant. It struck me odd there was so much coverage until I realized they all focused on the negativity of the war and ignored any good that was coming out of the contested invasion. You have to always look harder to find those articles. SGT Chapman knew of the war's positive aspects—his comrade-in-arms spoke of those positives at his funeral.

Every time I hear of a KIA, my thoughts are immediately of the family left behind. I know as long as there is a war, there will be KIA's. All have families that are dealing with the tough day-to-day coping with that loved one's death—and I know how long it will continue.

But I see a difference with this current war—the stigma that was prevalent during the Vietnam War is gone. People are not afraid to talk about this war, or wear their uniforms when traveling. There are support groups and agencies to help the returning wounded warriors. And the Vietnam veterans have made sure the returning troops are treated with honor and dignity. They vowed to not let history repeat itself.

I've witnessed Vietnam veterans buying a beer or lunch for returning troops at airport layovers. Mike has done it. Many times I've seen the airlines upgrade a uniformed vet to First Class when there was space available. And I've been fortunate to see the USO room at Atlanta's Hartsfield Airport being manned by the Atlanta Vietnam Veterans Business Association. They cater and dote on our military's young men and women, showing respect they never received upon their return from Nam over forty years ago.

Hard to believe the guys returning from Vietnam were told not to wear their uniform while traveling, knowing there were plenty of American who would say or do something, like spit on them, because of their participation in the much-hated war.

But I also know the similarities. There are losses—thousands of little sisters and brothers that are confused and hurting, and many of them will internalize their feelings. Some may even have questions, just like I did, because of a closed casket. So maybe reading about my journey could somewhat ease their pain.

Also, I don't know where I would be without the willingness of the Pink Panthers, who helped me understand what the last nine months of your life were like. Perhaps a veteran reading these letters will see how valuable his or her insight can be. Knowing your unit has not forgotten you is huge—and it is never too late for that.

And I think reading these letters might help the parents who have lost a child to war, who also have other children at home. It's not that Daddy and Mother were wrong. There were no how-to books dealing with grieving over a child lost to combat. The greatest generation, forever stoic—the way they thought they were supposed to be. Mother and Daddy wouldn't have accepted help from counselors or clergy. They closed up. Four decades later, we know holding in your emotions is, perhaps, not the best way to handle grief.

Speaking of holding in emotions... Daddy making that split-second decision to go on with Redina's wedding—this on the very day we received the telegram you were missing in action—was probably one of the hardest things he had ever done. I know it's not something everyone could do. But he did so—knowing that whatever the outcome, it shouldn't spoil the happiness Mike and Redina deserved. After all, it was their day! And I think that was the right decision.

I don't want to sound philosophical. Just wanted to tell you that I am thinking about sharing your letters—letters from my heart—because they may someday help someone else.

Somehow, I know you understand and approve.

Love, Susie

His life was short, why did it have to end?
Oh, what I would give to have him back again.

But I ran my fingers across his name,
and I could almost feel his pain.
I heard the gun fire, I saw him fall.
I touched his name upon The Wall.

—The Wall (I Touched His Name)
By Marie Zerby

QUESTIONS WITHOUT ANSWERS

Dear Mark,

Seems all my life I've wondered what you would look like, what you would have done with your life—what you might have said about what I have done with mine.

I've wondered if Daddy and Mother might have stayed together. Would Mother have still been sick half of her life? I'm sure all families have questions. These two questions will never have answers.

Whether you were for the war or against the war, after a loss, the war becomes the lesser part as you try to come to grips with life without them—that's the major part. Then there's isolation. Self imposed or people stayed away because they didn't know what to say or do.

One weekend when I lived in Virginia, we visited a Civil War battleground, The Battle of Bull Run, in Manassas. I remember looking out over the acres of green grass and rolling hills. A row of cannons at the ready. Old fences positioned like they might have been over a hundred years ago. I wandered off alone and stood by some trees to imagine the sounds of cannons and muskets. I didn't want to picture carnage the way it must have been. I thought about what we had studied in school—the reason they fought. But never really about the human aspect of it. Over six hundred thousand died. Families went to the battlefields to find their loved ones, bring them home and bury them. I admit I didn't give it too much thought when I was in junior high school. Now when I think about losing you, a family member—this is unfathomable. How did they do it? In the 1860's those families lost fathers, sons, sometimes more than one son, sometimes from both sides. Can you imagine it all depended on where you happened to live? The devastation must have been incomprehensible. But life went on—families rebuilt. Everyone around them was in the same situation. Everyone understood.

We weren't like that though—more like isolation. None of our neighbors were drafted and none of our neighbors were enlisting. We didn't know anyone who buried a son or father killed in the Vietnam War.

I felt like our parents never rebuilt. They never seemed to cling to each other for strength. It was as if they just muddled through life.

Mother and Daddy sold the house we grew up in the month after I graduated high school in '72. The next year they moved three thousand miles away and then several years later divorced. Sure Daddy remarried. But I never really saw a zest for life in him. Mother either.

They just went on.

Recently, I called Fort Benning and spoke to a Sergeant in the Army Casualty Mortuary and Affairs Office. I told her I was curious how they contact KIA families now. She was candid with me on phone about current protocol. The days of the family just being handed a telegram have ended. The military has made it critical to assist and care for the family of the fallen—available twenty-four hours a day. Looks like the military learned from mistakes made in the 40s during World War II, the 50s during the Korean War, the 60s and into the early 70s during the Vietnam War. What a shame a half million families were just handed a telegram during those three wars—and then they were abandoned.

When I looked up the phone number for Fort Benning I noticed what the military calls the money paid to the survivor after a combat death: Death Gratuity. Really? I leave a gratuity on a table in a restaurant to reward the wait-staff for a job well done. I give a valet attendant a gratuity when he brings me my parked car.

I know it's only a word, I know, but that word just seems wrong.

Didn't think you were going to get a little American history lesson, did you? Crazy stuff that pops into my head. Just goes to show that you pop into my head often. You are never very far from my thoughts.

Yeah, you pop into my thoughts a lot.

Your little sister, Susie

"…We have a simple view of war. We hate it; we see no glory in it; we grieve the suffering that results from it; but, as loyal and proud and patriotic Americans, by God, when our country calls we stand up, we show up, we fall in, we do our duty…"

—Maury Edmonds, MG (ret.) United States Army

JOE KLINE

Dear Mark,

Not long after I joined the Family Contacts Committee I was invited to be on The Vietnam Helicopter Flight Crew Network list server. It's a computerized mailing list for Vietnam War helicopter pilots and crew members. The purpose of my selection: if given a case to work on, I had immediate access to over three hundred veterans who may be able to help. That's a pretty good place to begin my search.

Some of the guys on the server are lurkers and never post a word. Some post every day. Then there are the regulars—retired guys who are on there most of the day. If I post about one of my cases and those guys don't know that KIA, it is possible they know someone who might. It's a great network of guys, always willing to lend a hand. They were very welcoming to Julie and me from day one. We are the only women on the net.

Shortly after joining the VHFCN, I went to the post office to pick up the mail from my P.O. box. We don't have mail delivery in our rural neighborhood. I pulled out a long tube and recognized the return label as one of the guys I knew from the net. Knew, means I hadn't met him in person but we know each other on the net and we conversed.

I sat down in my truck and opened the tube, cutting the tape with my pocket-knife. I got back out of my truck to unroll the white paper. I was stunned. It was a large, 20 X 28 color print of his painting of a team of Cobras in flight in Vietnam. The title of the print is Chariots of Fire. You would love it! Penciled at the bottom:

AH-1G Cobra Gunships of the 361ˢᵗ Aviation Co. (Escort) 'Pink Panthers' Kontum, Vietnam 1969.

In memory of CWO Mark Clotfelter, Killed-In-Action June 16, 1969

Joe Kline

To say I was surprised doesn't even come close. To make this even more special, Joe touched my heart by personalizing one of the Cobras. Up near the center, under the rotor blades, he hand-painted your Pink Panther unit patch—honoring you in the best way he knew, through his art.

Whenever I have posted a request to the guys on the net I always sign it:

Susan Clotfelter Jimison Proud Sister of Mark Clotfelter 361ˢᵗ Aviation Co. (Escort) —KIA June 16, 1969

So the guys know my story—which is really your story. From day one they understood. They get it. There haven't been many places I've been since 1968—back when you deployed to Vietnam—that people "get it." If the subject of Vietnam came up, and it was rare if it did, people didn't really understand it.

These guys do. They understand your courage. They understand your missions. They understand your sacrifice—and they understand mine. Their understanding is like no other.

When I reread what Joe wrote across the bottom of the print, I read between the lines. I know Joe and all these guys know—it could have been them.

I've since met Joe Kline. He was a door gunner with the Kingsmen, B Company, 101st Airborne Division, Air Assault. He's at every VHPA reunion, working in the vendor room. Always busy personalizing with their unit patch a print someone has purchased. Each reunion we attend, I stop by his booth to say hello. And when he sees me, he puts his paint brush down, removes his glasses, and comes out from behind his tables to give me a hug.

It isn't just that these guys all get it. I get it, too. I know they look at me and know how different it could have been.

I could be their little sister.

Your little sister, Susie

Sharing tales of those we've lost,
Is how we keep from really losing them.

- Mitch Albom

PAY IT FORWARD

Dear Mark,

Remember I've been working with a committee that helps people try to locate those who knew their loved one who died in Vietnam? Many are just beginning a search like Julie and I began in 1997. The reason Julie and I offer our help is because we know how much finding your Pink Panthers and David Kink's CAV unit means to us. We know that without the guys telling us stories and sharing their memories with us, the pain of loss would still be like it was in the late 60s. We were two little girls, our big brothers went away to war—and then they were gone forever. As we grew older we had more and more questions. No one was talking about the war or about you and David. So we kept it all bottled up until '97. Working on this committee is really just paying-it-forward.

I wanted to tell you about a case I worked on several years back. A young man wrote to the Family Contacts Committee with hope we could help him find someone who remembered the uncle he was named for, but whom he never met. The young man's name is Chriss Cabodi and his uncle, Chriss Roediger, was a Cobra pilot like you. Chriss felt like he needed to know the man he was named for and he was certain the men who knew him best were those who served with him in Vietnam.

And that's where I came in. I was assigned Case Number 322 and was forwarded the contact information, the incident report of helicopter number 68-15145, crash date October 8, 1969, and the unit information. Everything just fell into place, because the uncle was a helicopter pilot and those men are the Vietnam veterans I have the most contact with.

I was soon able to put Chriss in touch with the Redskins, Company D, 158th Assault Helicopter Battalion. Also, I found a few from the uncle's Flight Class, 68-6 who remembered his uncle well. Like finding the Pink Panthers, this search was quick and truly a success story.

However, I found a discrepancy in the incident report that apparently confused the first helicopter (68-15044) that had crashed that night with Chriss Roediger's (68-15145) crash that followed when he was sent out to locate that downed helicopter. The original incident report I was given said Chriss crashed and died because the rotor blade struck the side of a mountain. What really happened was:

> ...the tail rotor was hit by small arms fire. He lost anti-torque control, which caused the helicopter to spin. He tried to recover the main rotor blade and crashed. If anyone could have recovered the helicopter, it would have been him. He was a great pilot. His crash was definitely not pilot error."

That explanation was given to me by MAJ Jerry Chandler, U.S. Army Ret., and subsequently the history of the crash was updated. Finding the guys in the unit was good for Chriss, the nephew, but also for the sake of historical accuracy, with the corrected information on the crash. As you know, there is a difference between being shot down and pilot error.

The day the Redskins lost CPT Chriss Roediger, CPT James Luscinski and CW2 Robert Watkins was an expensive day for the unit with the loss of three lives and two aircraft. CW2 Watkins and the wreckage have never been located and thought to be along the border of Laos and South Vietnam.

Chriss and I communicated often with updates. It was great to hear about all the phone calls he had received and to hear how much he had learned about his uncle. We marveled at how open the Redskins were to talk to him about their past. He couldn't get over how much he learned from them in such a short time, and was very appreciative of my help.

...It meant a lot to me to hear how members of the unit saw Chriss as a role model and their big brother. Everything they have told me followed what my family has always said about what an amazing person he was. Sorry to write such a ridiculously huge message, but I wanted you to know how grateful I am for the time you've spent and the progress you've made on my behalf. I appreciate you contacting the database chairman of The Vietnam Helicopter Pilots Association with the correct information about the crash. Thanks again, for everything. I hope to leave you more messages about my correspondences."

He shared everything he learned with his mom, Chriss Roediger's sister, and his grandmother.

I mentioned to Chriss that I would be traveling to Washington D.C. in November, to read your name at The Wall for the 20th Anniversary. Because he lived in nearby McClean, Virginia, I suggested Chriss read his uncle's name. He sent in his request immediately. In a few weeks, he was notified that he would be able to read his uncle's name, and his list included CPT Cabodi's copilot, CPT James Luscinski. I was thrilled for him to have the honor to read the names, but also for the opportunity to meet him.

On Veterans Day weekend, we both arrived at The Wall early in the morning. I was delighted to meet this young man. Of all the cases I have worked on, I never had the opportunity to meet any of them face to face—until now.

I believe his uncle looked down upon the podium with great pride on that beautiful fall morning, immensely proud of the incredible young man his sister raised—his namesake.

The following May, Chriss mailed me a California newspaper article with a wonderful picture of his reflection with his mother in the black panel of the Moving Wall. The article tells how there was an online remembrance left on a virtual Vietnam Veterans Memorial page that prompted his search to try to find people who served with his uncle. Also in the article, his sister Leslye (and young Chriss's mother) reminisces, "He always got himself out of pinches. I had no thought that he'd be killed."

Wow, that really hit home.

So, I just wanted you to know that I have taken what I learned and who I have met and put it to good use! Not all cases are as successful as this one. But, if given the opportunity, I have to at least try.

I keep in touch with Chriss. He's a father now and has moved back to California. He continues to do research on his uncle, and now even his grandfather's military days. Kind of a military history buff. All this history will be passed on to that new little fellow someday.

Passing down our memories is how we keep you with us.

Love, Susie

...A picture's worth a thousand words
But you can't see what those shades
of gray keep covered
You should've seen it in color...
                    —In Color by Jamey Johnson

YOUR OLD '66

Dear Mark,

I know I've told you many times how I thought our family was the only ones who touched your name on The Wall in D.C. Then I told you how awesome I thought it was that the guys from your unit and flight class did, too. I admitted I was so wrong in thinking people had just moved on and forgotten you.

Today, I went online and looked up your name on the Vietnam Veterans Memorial Fund. It's the online version of the granite memorial in D.C. I've left a few pictures and remembrances on there in the past. To my surprise, there was a post under mine from a high school classmate of yours!

Some of us from Hialeah High School (classes 65–67) recall Mark. We'll never forget the sacrifice he made for us and the United States. His place on The Wall will keep a place in our memories forever. Myriad thanks. Dr. Pete Ciolfi

That was thoughtful of your classmate of nearly fifty years ago, to leave a remembrance. I got out your old musty smelling yearbooks and saw that Pete was in the class before you, graduating in '65. Since I had both the '66 and the '65 out, I thought I would look through them a little. All the black-and-white photos just look so sixties—bouffant hairdo's, saddle-oxford shoes and letter sweaters. The ink on the pages has faded with age and in many places, almost bled through the page. The plastic protector on the outside is brittle and cracked.

Loose, inside of old '66, is a blue booster ribbon for the football game against Miami Springs. Tucked neatly with it is the following morning's newspaper article that says Hialeah won—your handwriting on the top corner, 11-18-65. It sure must have been a big deal.

Hialeah High School doesn't have to win another football game this season. It beat Miami Springs Friday night 13-6, at Hialeah Stadium before a crowd of 6,500. Angered by seven straight defeats, Hialeah's senior linemen teamed with its sophomore backs to crush the Golden Hawks in the first game of what may become the county's most fierce neighborhood rivalry.

Reading page after page of what classmates wrote to you, one girl wrote you were "such a camera bug" and another girl said "to a sweet guy who treats a girl like a lady." Those brought smiles to my face even though I never knew those girls. Geometry must have been a fun class, because more than one mentioned all the laughter and good times in class.

There's Redina on page 186—I have never seen this picture! I'd forgotten she was a sophomore when you were a senior. Because she was in the marching band I am sure she was at that football game, too.

Our neighbor, Lynn Wildman , who, a few years after graduation, painted the helicopter caricatures on your VW van, drew a perfect rendition of a horse in your yearbook. Not sure if it was because the family owned and loved horses or because that was our Hialeah High School mascot, the thoroughbred. Lynn is a natural-born artist.

But what I read the most were the many, well-meaning wishes of "the best of luck—good luck in the future."

Makes me sad—your luck ran out.

Love, Susie

Every American generation needs to understand that, regardless of the controversy over whether we should have been in Vietnam or whether we should not have been in Vietnam, those who served there—who answered the call to duty and served so far from home and family—did what they were asked to do and more, and did it in the face of tremendous danger and sacrifice. They were noble warriors and they deserve the Nation's respect, recognition and gratitude. There's another group that never gets the recognition they deserve. They're our families who stayed behind, who were consumed with fear and uncertainty about our safety but who carried on supporting us and the rest of our families. We owe them more than we can describe.

—Maury Edmonds, MG (ret.) United States Army

FIT FOR A MUSEUM

Dear Mark,

I just want to tell you something. When I requested your DD 201 file, which contains all you records with the military—from induction in Coral Gables, Florida, to basic training to Vietnam—it also contained your DD 214, the most important of all military records: your performance files, and flight hours. But I also received a complete set of your medals. Mother has your medals, the originals, so I started thinking about what I would do with all the new ones, which even have your name engraved on the back of each one. Stuffing them in one of my drawers serves no purpose. Passing them down? To whom? I guess I could, but then they would be stuffed into someone else's drawer!

There's a new museum under construction, a mile down the street from Fort Wolters, in Mineral Wells, Texas. You know, where you learned to first fly a helicopter. I've met the museum personnel at reunions and the project is moving along nicely. One of the newest additions is a Huey mounted on a steel structure, on an angle, giving it the appearance of being in flight.

I purchased a brick personalized with your name and unit and it's been placed in their Memory Garden along with hundreds of others. They have also built a half-scale Vietnam Veterans Memorial—identical to the one in Washington, D.C.

Your name is on the replicated Camp Holloway Wall, the one that has the names of all who were lost from that base— also an exact replica of the memorial in Vietnam.

See? You're already connected with this place!

The mission of the museum is simple: To promote an understanding of the Vietnam era while honoring those who served. So, I thought the perfect thing to do with your new medals would be to donate them to the museum. When I mentioned it to the guys on the VHFCN, John Grow, a Texan, offered to mount and frame them for me. How nice! Extra nice, because he knew the protocol of the order in which they should be positioned, none of which I did.

I also had a brass plate made that says:

Mark D. Clotfelter
Class 68-9 Ft. Rucker
Chief Warrant Officer
361ˢᵗ Company (Escort)
The Pink Panthers
Cobra Pilot
KIA 6-16-69

In retrospect, I should have put CWO in front of your name. I just didn't know any better at the time.

I have to tell you, it turned out wonderful. More than wonderful! Truly fit for a museum. John Grow has a framing business and really knows his stuff! I sent him an 8 x 10 professional color photo of you in your Class A dress greens wearing the aviator wings you earned, plus the brass plate and all of your medals. He mounted them so beautifully. Green suede-like matting with double-matted cutouts for everything. It's pretty big, too—23 x 25. All in a nice cherry-colored, wooden frame. Everything is perfect. First Class.

I hope many people go and bring their children to the museum to learn. Schools across the country have skipped over much of the Vietnam War in history class. It's almost as if it's up to the parents now to educate their children on our own country's history.

Your picture and medals will hang in The National Vietnam War Museum once they get the building completed. I'm holding onto them until it's ready. It's strange, but I can't place them on our wall because I feel like they already belong to the museum.

It truly is the best way I could honor you and all the medals you earned. The museum is a more appropriate place for them to be displayed, instead of collecting dust somewhere. Whoever I would have handed them down to can see them in Texas.

Funny, for years it was almost like a secret. Nobody talked about you or the war. Then when I found your unit, it seems that's all I talked about for a while. Now, I am ready to share you with the world. Well, whoever walks through the doors of that museum.

I look forward to the day I take your medals to Mineral Wells, Texas. You know how proud I am of you—now all the museum visitors will see some of the reasons why.

Love, Susie

You haven't seen a tree
Until you have seen its shadow
From the sky.

—Amelia Earhart

WOP-WOP-WOP

Dear Mark,

I finally did it—I flew in a helicopter! The Vietnam Dustoff Association was in town for their annual reunion and member Steve Vermillion let me know about the opportunity to fly in a Huey. I told Mike and he said *you should do it!* With almost fifteen-thousand hours flying helicopters he wasn't going to go for the ride, but wanted me to. He kind of laughed and said he never paid to ride in one, he has always been paid to fly them.

Just outside Dobbins Air Reserve Base in Marietta, the Dustoff group and Mike and I gathered at 10 a.m on Saturday. We were given safety instructions, ear-plugs, signed our waivers, and waited to hear that wop-wop-wop of the Huey approaching. Soon, miles out, not yet in sight, we could hear it. Mike said, "the NVA could hear us coming—just like this—and had plenty of time to get ready to shoot it down." That was a heart-stopping thought for me. No wonder there were over five-thousand helicopters destroyed during the war. You might not know where the enemy was—but the enemy could always hear you coming.

Huey 68-16104 had everyone's attention from the approach to the landing. The wind it stirred up was more than I had expected. I quickly wondered why I had bothered taking the time to style my hair this morning.

You'd be interested in the history of this aircraft. It was built in 1968 and immediately went to Vietnam, flew with the 191st Assault Helicopter Company, and A Company 229th Assault Helicopter Battalion and then returned to the United States

206 | Dear Mark

in 1972. After a few years at Rucker, it flew many years with
the Alabama National Guard. It's still owned by the Army but
is on loan to the Army Aviation Heritage Foundation located
right here in Georgia. They are all very seasoned pilots and
crew who donate their time for the cause. With the love you
had for aviation and particularly the Cobra, I know you would
love to have been a part of this group! They do have Cobras,
but didn't bring them because the cost of riding in one was
five-hundred dollars. There weren't any takers for that steep
fee!

My instructions from Mike were: Don't sit backwards—
don't sit by the open doors. Was he afraid I might fall out? Or
maybe he was worried it would scare me.

So, I was the first one in and sat facing forward, directly in
the middle. As it turned out it was perfect. It was the only seat
I could stretch my long legs out—and had the best view of the
cockpit. The pilot and co-pilot were dressed in Army green
flight suits and wore helmets. It wasn't hard to imagine it being
you and Mike sitting up there.

Everyone else, Steve Vermillion included, was getting buck-
led in and checked for the tightness of their belts. I was ready
and was just taking it all in. The smell, color of the metal, so
many knobs and gauges, and then the sound I'd heard for so
many years out of Daddy in his airplane—CLEAR! The pilot
was ready to crank the engine and wanted everyone to know
the blades were going to start moving. We were about to take
off!

I knew we weren't going to rumble down the runway like
in an airplane, but it was a little surprising how effortlessly it
was to lift off the ground in a forward motion. Not surprising
though, was how loud it was. I had ear-plugs in my hand but
I didn't want to miss anything—not from any moment of this
flight. I never put them in my ears.

The scenery of Kennesaw Mountain was luscious green. I
imagined the lusciousness of Vietnam—before Agent Orange
was sprayed to defoliate the trees. The enemy could hide any-

where and just wait to shoot these helicopters out of the sky. I wondered what the other passengers were thinking about— while I was thinking about you flying in Vietnam. I looked over my right shoulder and saw the mount for a machine gun. I thought about the thousands of rounds of ammunition that had been fired from right there to protect our guys on the ground, trudging through jungle or in a hot landing zone.

Maybe because the doors were off, maybe because it was a helicopter, it just didn't feel as safe as in Daddy's airplanes. I wasn't scared, but the openness gave me a sense of vulnerability.

The pilot made some turns and dips. What an amazing feeling of lightness, like we were floating. All while the wind is blowing my hair and the rotor blades are making the wop-wop sound.

That wop-wop-wop has always caused me to pause and look up whenever I hear it. No matter where I am. There has always been this simultaneous thought whenever I've heard the sound of any helicopter approaching—and that is of you. I want you to know though, they aren't bad thoughts. I think of you because I know how much you loved flying them. When I hear any helicopter off in the distance I try my best to find it. When I see it and I'm looking to the sky, I always think of you and smile.

It was great today, to finally fly in a helicopter—I would do it again in a heartbeat.

Pretty dang cool!

Love, Susie

In war, there are no unwounded soldiers.

—José Narosky, Argentinean writer

DADDY'S WAR

Dear Mark,

Eighteen years ago a reporter from the local newspaper came to Daddy's house to interview him. The War Birds were coming to town on their annual trek, possibly their last one. The B-17 and B-24 would arrive at the Bremerton Airport in Washington State that weekend and Daddy would volunteer his time to give "tours," just like he had done for the past several years. It was important to him to educate younger Americans about what he knew about the B-24 he helped crew in 1943. That year was the fiftieth anniversary of the end of World War II.

The reporter, Ben Keenan, got more out of Daddy in that one interview than I ever knew of his war-time exploits. For that reason I have kept, and treasured, this newspaper article. The article Daddy never ever mentioned.

I knew he was a waist-gunner/radio man and was stationed on the island of Morotai in the South Pacific. I knew he flew thirty-three combat missions—but only because Mother told me.

In the Editor's Column the title read: Looking Back for Inspiration

>...*From the distance of decades, his service appears as simple and straightforward as the meticulously kept logs he still has of the thirty-three missions he flew, bombing Japanese shipping, fuel plants, and runways.*
>
>*But as he talks, you realize there is a lot more to it. His eyes grow damp as he remembers witnessing one plane's bombs hit a plane from another squadron.*

"On some missions, the plane had to fly straight and level for a long time before it comes to its target. That's when they shot flak at you. There were black clouds everywhere," he recounts. "You'd tell yourself 'If I ever get back, I promise I'll never do this again. But after a day or two, you got over it and went out again."

I ask him why he always went out again. It takes a long time for him to answer. When he does, I get the impression he's showing me something of great value.

"After what happened at Pearl Harbor, I would do just about anything to help win that war," he says.

It wasn't just him. The whole country felt the same way. People haven't been that together since then.

So many times I have wondered what you knew. Sometimes I think about when you were home on leave, maybe having a beer, and if Daddy might have talked about his war. But I don't think so. Pretty sure he would have thought you were too young and wouldn't understand. Maybe he was waiting until you came home. Then you would understand.

He used to get up early Sunday mornings and drive to Uncle Coston's, have coffee and sometimes talk about the war. Aunt Arlene thought it was good for both of them. Many times she would just stay in bed longer so they could chat. If she got up, the conversation would always change.

A few months after Daddy was gone, I ran into Spider, an old friend of his. They used to meet at nine every morning with other retired men for coffee and to chat. It was the same crowd every day. Then, as if someone blew a whistle at ten a.m. sharp, they would rise, put their ball caps on and head to the post office around the corner. They knew everyone's mail would be stuffed into their boxes by ten. Picking up their mail was just something to do for these retirees.

Spider told me he always believed Daddy's tales of war and said all the others guys just made theirs up. He said he still misses "Red" at coffee every morning. It made me feel good that Daddy was able to talk to someone about his war. And that Spider still thinks of him.

I wish Daddy had written his memories down. He kept his emotions intact, his deepest hurts hidden. Our past is what molds us into who we are, and if we had known more, we kids would not have questioned the why's.

His memories died with him and perhaps that is what he had planned.

Love, Susie

The natural progression of life is death, but that doesn't mean we like it or are prepared to lose people so interwoven in our lives. Ken's cancer was brutal and predictable. And so sad. Ken arrived at the 361st in Vietnam after we lost you. He was there with my Mike in 1970. But that doesn't matter. The Panthers, whether they knew you or not, treat me as one of their own. Ken was no different. Sometimes I forget who knew you and who didn't.

A few years back, Ken had unit pins made. It was a rendition of the Pink Panther, lying down—smoking a cigar. He handed them out to all of us at the reunion that summer and they were a hit. Most of the guys immediately put them on their ball-caps. I still remember Ken handing me two in an elevator.

Following his surgery, I'd drop him a note occasionally to ask how he was. Told him I was just checking in. Every time the reply was the same: Once again all is well. And he would add: *See you in Louisville,* where the next reunion will be.

I fell for his responses because I wanted to believe it was true.

Ken was fun. I imagine he was always the life of the party in his younger days. Pretty sure he'd always lived life to the fullest. I can still see him every 4th of July—his white hair and Fu-Manchu painted red, white and blue. Like I said, Ken was fun.

Next summer in Louisville we will toast those we've lost. Those lost in Vietnam like you and those lost since. Like Paul Riley and Ken Otto.

Love, Susie

Major Rodgers would again have to ease my anguish with the loss of Mark Clotfelter and Michael Mahowald in July. His words—with their salving effect—I wrote down and keep in my office to this day: "Wrap today's sadness in a small package, and lose it among tomorrow's projects."
—Gary Higgins, Tales From SOG, Secret War and its Secret Heroes "The Bra"

PRECISE MOMENT

Dear Mark,

I flew into the Sea-Tac airport last week for a seven day visit. I moved from the Seattle area four years ago and was looking forward to seeing family and friends. After I picked up my bag from the luggage carousel, I headed towards the exit doors to find the new light train to Seattle. I stopped to attach my computer case to the handle of my rolling bag. As I was positioning my luggage I noticed a gathering of people. There was a lot of chatter, camouflage colored balloons and a sign that read "Welcome Home Sgt Rice." Another sign said "Welcome Home Uncle Mark."

The first thing that went through my mind was: is this what it would have looked like had you come home forty-four years ago? Is this what we missed—what should have been? I was frozen, just standing there staring. I wondered what war their Uncle Mark was coming home from. Afghanistan? Iraq?

I felt out of place because I didn't know these people or the man they anxiously awaited. I felt like an intruder. No one else was just standing there like me.

Tears began to well in my eyes; I knew I had to leave. I turned to go and as cheers and excitement erupted to a much louder level, I walked faster to not see the very thing I was compelled to stand and watch just moments ago.

I don't think anyone in that crowd noticed I was there. Their attention was focused on that escalator, not wanting to miss the precise moment they saw their "Mark" come into view.

I really was happy for them, and at the same time, very sad for the thousands of Gold Star families that had missed that precise moment.

As you can see—every once in a while something happens, out-of-the-clear-blue, that reminds me of you. It isn't always sad. I don't want you to think that. There's many times a happy or funny memory will cross my mind and brings a smile to my face. Today though, I had a moment of sadness for you—and for me—for that precise moment we never had.

Love, Susie

> ...I learned to keep some space between fellow comrades and myself during combat. This allowed me to accept whatever fate was handed out, without a deep emotional sense of loss.
>
> —Robert Steen, Panther 11

ROSS CLEMENT

Dear Mark,

I just got off the phone with a flight school classmate of yours, Ross Clement. For years now he calls and checks in a couple of times a year. He said he's been reminiscing, thinking about you and decided to call.

We caught up on what we are both doing these days. He is still flying. And I caught him up on what I was doing.

We always talk about you, too. And the guys you both knew. I told him Ralph Chappell wrote me about spending time with you in Basic Training and then Flight School and how he hoped I knew you were in love with flying. Said you had a passion for it. He also said because you were accepted in Cobra school meant you did well in Flight School—better than average because those were the ones going to Hunter Army Airfield. Ross could tell I enjoyed these emails about you and just let me ramble on about it.

I brought up the letter you sent me in '68 when you were stationed at Hunter Army Air Field in Savannah. I asked if he was one of the guys you roomed with there. He said no, because he didn't go to Cobra Transition School. He flew Huey's with the Sharks in Vietnam. So we kicked around who it might have been.

Because I still have the letters you sent me, I have the address for the house you lived in. I even have a few pictures you took. What a grand house it is! I love the huge Southern-style wrap-around porch. When I get to Savannah, I'll see if I can find the house. It shouldn't be too hard.

It's always good to hear from Ross. He always invites us to visit Alaska.

Makes me happy to know, once again, you're remembered.

Love, Susie

> …We should never forget our fallen because the families have not. They earned the right for us to remember.
> —Mike Sloniker, LTC U.S. Army (retired)

GOLD STAR FAMILY BREAKFAST

Dear Mark,

Five of us Gold Star sisters attended the VHPA reunion in Dallas. All of our brothers had been pilots in different units in Vietnam. We gathered for breakfast early one morning downtown at The Pearl Street Café to get to know each other. It was 2004, and this became our first annual Gold Star Family Breakfast.

It was quite informal as we went around the table introducing ourselves and it soon became apparent we had shared similar paths. We all had feared our search for someone who might remember our brothers could be a painful reminder of memories better off locked away. We all experienced quite the opposite.

"The men our brothers loved have come to love us, and what we all share can bring us together in a way no other relationship can match," Julie said that day.

When we got ready to leave, we asked for the bill. The waitress smiled and said the Blue Stars had paid for our breakfast. They wanted her to pass on a message to us: "Enjoy your breakfast, from your brothers." Sherry Leeper's brother Wally had been a Blue Star, a member of the 48th Attack Helicopter Company. One Blue Star sister and they paid for all of our meals? We were all totally stunned.

The following year, the reunion was in San Francisco. Julie and I planned the second annual Gold Star Family Breakfast at Mel's Drive-in Diner across the street from the hotel, on Van Ness. We walked there the day after we arrived to check it out. We needed to make sure that our table would accommodate ten people. This time we had a few VHPA members requesting to join us with their wives, and our Family Contacts Committee Chair, Gary Thewlis, and a Gold Star wife.

That evening, as Julie and I were waiting for a hotel elevator, Blue Star member Rick Lester came up to us and said a collection was taken up during the Cabaret that evening. A few of the guys were talking about the Gold Star Family breakfast the next morning and on the spur of the moment they passed a hat around. They all agreed the families should not have to pay for their breakfast. They wanted the family members to feel welcomed and embraced. Rick was holding a large brown paper lunch bag, choked at the top with his hand. We were truly surprised and thanked Rick—more than once. We then said our good-byes as we got in the elevator. Once the door closed and the elevator began to move, Julie peeked in the top of the bag. She had a funny expression on her face. I said, "What?" Speechless, she stepped closer and let me peek, too. The sack was stuffed to the top with dollar bills. Ones—fives—tens—twenties. We could see there was way more money in that bag than we would need for one breakfast. When the doors of the elevator opened, Julie clutched the bag tight.

Safely inside our locked hotel room, Julie stood at the dresser with the lamp on and counted the money—laying it out in separate piles of one hundred. Every time she got to one hundred, she looked up in disbelief. Seven hundred dollars later, we were shocked at the generosity—from many who didn't even know us.

Thankfully, there was a safe in our room!

The next morning we walked to Mel's Drive-In to meet up with the eight others that had confirmed with us. We all arrived at the same time, as if it were choreographed.

Like the previous year, we went around the table and introduced ourselves. All Gold Star sisters told of whom they had lost, how old they were then, and a little about finding their brother's unit.

Julie shared her thoughts on the years gone by:

Each of us KIA family members bore the pain of our losses with a certain stoicism brought on by the fact that in those days, no one—not even our own family members—wanted to talk about Vietnam. I have been told by many of my "new brothers" that when veterans came home from the war, they just put Vietnam "on the shelf." So did the family members. We usually lacked information about the circumstances of our loved one's death and knew no way to find answers should we be ready to face them.

All that has changed for us now that we have found our brother's units.

One of the veterans who joined us was Gary Rossome, Ghostrider 17, complete with his Black Cav hat. He wanted to share a poem from *The Price of Exit* by Tom Marshall. Gary felt it was appropriate because it was written by Gold Star Mother, Mrs. Evelyn Hatley.

…There's no remains, no grave to be, nothing except sweet memories.
A picture of him is left instead, a folded flag to show he's dead.
Always I'll look at the smiling face, of the picture I hold here in his place.
Always I'll hold in grief and strife, this flag as if it were my life.
Always a Gold Star Pin I'll wear, in memory of a life so sweet and fair.
A picture, a flag, and a Gold Star Pin, I'll hold in the place of him.

Everyone at the table personally related to her poem. Perfectly titled: *A Picture, A Flag and a Gold Star Pin*. Mrs. Hatleys' son had been a Phoenix, a sister company of the Ghostriders. C Company, 158 Attack Helicopter Battalion, with the 101st Airborne (Airmobile) Division. Sadly, her son Joel's remains, and all those on board that day, had not been found when she wrote the poem. However, October 5, 1990, nineteen years later, in a single flag-draped coffin at Arlington National Cemetery, all those on board 67-1734 were finally laid to rest. I've always said it would have been worse, for all of us—to not know—to have to wait for remains to be sent home.

When it came time to pay the bill, Julie made the announcement that the entire breakfast was being paid for by VHPA member donations. Everyone was so surprised by the generosity.

Julie went home that summer and opened a special account at the bank, because she was now accountable for the unexpected donation that would be used the following year.

So, for the past nine years the Gold Star Family Breakfast has continued. VHPA members still donate money but now instead of passing a black CAV hat, or a paper lunch sack, the Executive Committee has embraced Gold Star family members like never before. They have added the annual breakfast to the registration form. VHPA members can choose when they register for the reunion to donate or not.

It's become tradition for Gary Rossomme to read Mrs. Hatley's poem, and now he gives the invocation. The Breakfast has grown from five to over sixty-five attending since we began in Texas in 2004.

We now meet in one of the banquet rooms inside the reunion hotel. We have veterans joining us, so our breakfast is early and we finish just in time for them to attend the annual business meeting.

Although the breakfast has grown, we never lose sight of the reason we're there. It's our time to share with others the ones we lost—the ones we're so proud of.

The reason we're at the VHPA reunion.

We each bring a picture of our loved one and display them on a table. Again, it just makes it more real when you can put a face to the name. Some of us wear our Gold Star pins.

I still think about you every day and always wish things had been different.

Love, Susie

I was the youngest child, so I got away with more.
I guess she was tired by the time I came along,
she'd laugh until she cried.
I could do no wrong, she would always save me,
Because I was her baby.

—Blake Shelton, Baby

JANUARY 24, 2014

Dear Mark,

Mother has an infection that sent her to the hospital. Dang, infections and fevers are so hard on old people. Mother's ninety-one now and so frail. Mike and I drove up so Redina didn't have to do everything alone. We took turns being there at the hospital and then the same at the rehabilitation center she was transferred to. Physical Therapy has their work cut out for them, as does Mother.

Mike, Redina, and my Mike and I were having dinner the other night, following a day spent with Mother. Jimison was talking about how he didn't letter in high school, he drove his Dad's car and never had a cheerleader for a girlfriend. But when he got into Army Aviation, life changed for him. He found he was good at flying. It was a huge confidence booster. So much so it was visible. He had found his niche in life.

Redina's Mike was quick to say that was not your story. He never saw a day that you did not show confidence. He recalled meeting you in the aviation program at Miami-Dade Junior College. Soon you were able to help Mike get a job at Aerodex where the main purpose there was rebuilding Pratt & Whitney J-57 engines used in F-4's and B-52's flying in Vietnam. He said you were a "nineteen year old inspector who exuded confidence." He was not surprised at all that you became a self reliant and very capable Cobra pilot.

We also talked about the Christmas gifts you sent to us in '68. I told Redina I still have the two ivory figurines—one, a lion sitting on black painted wood and the other, an ivory Vietnamese fishing vessel on matching wood. I'm pretty sure it's ivory but it could be bone. I've kept them and treasured them for over forty years because you gave them to me. I didn't ever give much thought to what they were made of. It never really mattered. What mattered was it was a present from you.

Redina still has the pair of black Asian lacquer vases you gave her that Christmas.

Mother is going to have to work hard to get back on her feet—to get back home in Redina's care. We talked about that, too. Linda is flying in on Friday to help out because I have to get back to Georgia. We encourage Mother, we push her in our own way but she is pretty stubborn. I wish you were here to encourage her, too. She may have listened to you more than us.

When we left the rehab center yesterday to get on the road to come home, Mother asked Jimison if he thought he would see ninty-one. He chuckled and said his Mom will be ninety-three next week, so maybe!

Every time I leave Mother these days, I never know if I will ever see her again. But she's surprised me so many times in the last several years. Fractured hip. Fractured pelvis. Pneumonia. Julie frequently reminds me old people will surprise you every time. So I carry that thought in my heart when I leave. It's still hard. I don't say good-bye. It's always, "I'll see you soon. I'll be back!"

I could never remember our parting word, yours and mine. I can't remember that day at all and I never knew why. So Redina and I talked about that, too. She said the reason I don't remember is you left before we got up for school that day. Wow, forty-five years later I find out why I can't remember saying goodbye to you—because I never had the chance.

I've always envied the picture Julie has of herself, her brother, and her Mom at the airport the day her brother David left. We should have had a picture like that, too. We could have said, "I'll see you soon" instead of goodbye—like I always do with Mother.

Talking about you after dinner the other night brought back some good memories. Not all good this time, but at least I now know why I can't remember.

We all wish things had been different.

Love, Susie

And now I'm glad I didn't know
The way it all would end,
the way it all would go
Our lives are better left to chance
I could have missed the pain,
but I'd have had to miss the dance.

—Garth Brooks

HELPFUL SUSIE

Dear Mark,

Hello old friend. It's Jaime,[1] Panther 21, 2nd platoon leader and RLO Mike Jimison. I'm trying to write this letter for your sister (my wife) without stumbling over too many words on her computer. Bet you never would have guessed I'd be doing this. I wouldn't have guessed it, either. Suz has spent a lot of time writing these letters to you. And I guess I've never really stopped thinking about you ever since that day in '69 at Camp Holloway when Mike Mahowald took my place in the front seat of our Cobra. It's weird how some things just never fade away—it's been almost 45 years now, and I can still see it. No telling how many lives were changed because of that day in '69.

Even if I wanted it to fade away, I don't think it would. It's like an old movie reel in my head that never stops playing. And it's not that I don't want to see the movie, but God knows I wish I could have changed the ending...

The day before everything changed forever was like every other day. After hours of flying, we got back to Holloway late. I scrawled the next day's schedule on the Plexiglas in grease pencil, blasted off for the showers and a steak at the O-Club. Halfway across the flight line, Mahowald stopped me and said he had breezed through his check-ride and familiarization

---

1 Jaime is a nickname given to Mike Jimison when he first got to Vietnam. Pronounced "Hi-me"

flight in the AO and couldn't wait to fly. If you remember, he arrived in country the same day as I did, but I got my check-ride first because I was senior. There was so much enemy activity up north around Dak To—we didn't have enough aircraft to spare for check rides and training. Every flyable aircraft we had was out flying every day. So, for six weeks, Mahowald filled sandbags around the hooches and helped build revetments on the ramp for aircraft parking, waiting for an available aircraft. I know it especially sucked for Mike because he was a licensed pilot before he joined the Army and couldn't wait to get out there. I felt bad because I told him that the schedule was already made out, but I'd make sure he got on the schedule the day after. I also told him he could ask around to the other pilots and see if they could use a day off. I was pretty sure somebody would let him take his place in the co-pilot's seat. Midway through dinner and after a couple of beers, there's Mike again asking if I'd found anyone who needed the day off. Again, I explained that it was up to him to ask around if he wanted to fly the next day.

Bright and early the next morning, standing outside Operations, there stood Mike with his helmet bag. I thought he had found a ride, but he wasn't even wearing a Nomex flight suit. He hadn't found anyone to swap with and wanted to make one last try this morning. I can still see him standing in front of me. Mike was a nice guy, loved to fly, fresh out of flight school, and ready to strap on the Cobra gunship, the newest and "baddest" gun platform in the Army's inventory. Who could blame him? We were all like that when we started out, and he was determined to fly that day. Finally, he convinced me that I needed a trip to the P.X. for toothpaste because I had flown almost every day for six weeks. I loaned him my Nomex shirt—name tag and rank included—and he jumped in my seat. Your front seat. You must have wondered what was playing out—but you never said a word. I knew it wouldn't matter to you because six weeks earlier, I was the new guy, assigned to fly with you, Panther 28, in your front seat on my first flight in country. I knew you wouldn't care if it were Mike's first flight. The two of you took off, ready to go to work.

Except that afternoon, word got back to the company area that you had been shot down. The first thing required was to check the operations schedule to determine who was on board the aircraft. There it was, in yellow grease pencil on the official Plexiglas flight assignment board, Clotfelter/Jimison. Paperwork had to be done in triplicate; replacement aircraft had to be requisitioned, infantry sent in to secure the area, the aircraft recovered, and next of kin notification had to be initiated. I snarled up the whole process when I walked in and erased my name from the board in operations with a swipe of my sleeve. I had forgotten to do it that morning. Communication was so bad back to the States that I didn't want Mom and Dad to be misinformed that I was MIA. I knew if the letters were already sent out, I couldn't have stopped them. I learned almost thirty years later how those letters had affected your family. Days passed before they could get to your wreckage because the NVA fought very hard to keep that piece of property along the road to Ben Het. We needed that road to move desperately needed supplies and they wanted to prevent that.

Eventually the Graves Registration unit was able to get in there and start the recovery on July 2nd. Sure enough, my Nomex on Mike got the whole documentation process rolling again of who was in the aircraft.

No, I'll never forget that day. "Shot down" is all we heard about the crash, no details whatsoever. I'll always wonder if you got hit and, because it was Mike's first day as co-pilot, he didn't know to grab the controls to fly it out of there. In the front seat of the aircraft, where Mike was, all he had was that little mirror on the window frame to check and see if the Aircraft Commander was all right in the back. If it were a catastrophic event like an engine, transmission, or tail-rotor failure—low level in the trees, it probably wouldn't have made any difference, but I'll always wonder if my experience might have meant I could have reacted faster and gotten us out of there. I won't know, but I'll always wonder.

It should have been me that day—me and you. Instead, it was you and Mike Mahowald.

You two were snatched from our presence that day but not from our memories.

The day you and Mike were killed was hell, but the truth is not all my memories of Vietnam are bad ones. Being in combat definitely heightened my senses and seared the sounds and smells forever in my mind. I believe the experience made me a better man, but I also found pushing the limits in Vietnam doesn't always translate well into civilian life. It's easy to drive too fast, drink too much, and get in the boss's face too often.

"Bullet proof" is not a good way to conduct life or relationships.

The people who are the most important in our lives, who never experienced what we did—our families—can never understand what makes us so different now. War changed us.

Mark, I am sorry to tell you our return to the U.S. wasn't any different from our send-off. After all these years, I can bury the hatchet with the protesters and the peaceniks, though I still have issues with draft dodgers who gave up their U.S. citizenship and went to Canada. They were allowed to come home and their citizenships were restored. Personally, I think they should have had been made to stick with their decision and loyalties like we had to. That leaves the three people whom I'll never be able to forgive or forget. One was a veteran of Vietnam who came home and trashed all the Vietnam vets and lied about his service, the second was whoever decided "ham and lima beans" sounded tasty for a C-ration selection, and the last is Jane Fonda. The first came very close to being elected as the President of the United States, but should have been tried for treason instead. Jane was nominated as one of the top 100 women in America. And I hope the C-rations guy was strung-up! Oh, how times have changed from our fathers' war.

After Vietnam, some of us continued flying. I'm sure you would have, too. Unfortunately, pay wasn't that good because there were thousands of us Vietnam-era pilots looking for flying jobs. The Army had produced thousands of pilots each month for rotation to Vietnam. The market was flooded, and the few businessmen needing us could pick and choose. Initially, we veterans were all referred to as "baby killers" and "drug addicts" on our return. For pilots, we were called "a dime a dozen" and "all the drunks in the gutters of New Orleans" by some of the more unscrupulous owners of companies hiring helicopter pilots. We just wanted to fly.

Some of the pilots gave up their dream to stay in the air and went back to school or took a job doing something else, anything to put food on the table. Their lives probably weren't so thrilling, but in the long run, they may have made the better decision. Still, they never got the chance to turn a blade again.

Whether we flew again or not, thousands of us turn up every year to an annual Vietnam Helicopter Pilots Association (VHPA) convention that rotates between major cities that have large enough hotels to handle a convention of 1,500 rowdy pilots who want to relive the peak year of their youth, renew friendships, and drink beer. They always play the songs of the times at the reunion, but on one occasion, Eric Burdon, who sang probably the most popular song in Vietnam, *We Gotta Get Outta this Place*, was the entertainment for the dance and banquet. When we recognized the beginning notes of that song, a couple thousand guys jumped up and sang it word-for-word at the top of their lungs, some with tears streaming down their cheeks. It was great, but sad in a way, too. Remember when we were kids and were introduced to a WWII or Korean Vet? We thought they were old, out of shape, dumpy, maybe looked like they should be teaching high school chemistry or filing taxes. Now that's us.

I know if I look hard enough, I can still see that fighting spirit. We may be grandpas now, but no one can ever take that spirit away from us.

 Truthfully, Mark, I don't care if we ever get recognized for our service in Vietnam. For me, it was always about the privilege to be accepted as part of a team that I could trust. The politicians are starting to come around to their error in the treatment we received and only now, after 45 years, can they see their mistake.

As far as I'm concerned, they didn't give a damn about us then, so I really don't believe them now.

I'm proud I served in Vietnam. We killed the enemy before they killed us. I fought for my friends who kept me alive and for my country, in that order. Pride and a paycheck lured me into the Army, but the friendships and camaraderie in the military taught me patriotism and honor.

I wish it had turned out different, Mark. Every day, I wish you were here. You and all your brothers-in-law would have made a great crew. You would have finally had brothers in your family, but you know I love all of your sisters. Each one has her own style and personality, and all are positive members in their family and community. You'd be proud of them. My favorite, of course, is "helpful" Susie as she was nicknamed by you and your sisters. The childhood name remains and it's accurate.

When she asked me to write this letter, I thought that Suz was kidding—I don't know how to do that. Now that I'm about to wrap this up, I realize that this was as much for me as it was for you.

Helpful Susie strikes again.

Until we meet again,

Panther 21 ... out

> "You look back on some little decision you made and realize all the things that happened because of it, and you think to yourself "if only I'd known, "but, of course, you couldn't have known."
> —Mary Downing Hahn, December Stillness

MY NEXT CHAPTER

Dear Mark,

It's 2014, and oh brother—I'll be 60 years old this year. It is hard for me to believe. Your birthday is just around the corner and this year you would have been 67.

Growing old is something you never got to do. For that reason alone I need to embrace it and not complain about graying hair and sagging skin. Growing old is a privilege the living take for granted.

Mother is doing fine. Once again, she had pneumonia, went to the hospital and rehab and is back home with Redina and Mike. It's where she wants to be. Strange, but she is eating better than she has in the last thirty years. We don't understand it, but we are looking forward to her crossing the ninety-pound mark on the scale.

Mike and I will celebrate our eighth wedding anniversary this summer. It always seems like so much longer because we've been together fifteen years. The day we got married in '06, I remember thinking I hope the 3rd time is a charm! Mike was probably thinking the same thing.

We both know we wouldn't be married had things been different June 16, 1969. If you had come home, there would have been no reason for me to search for your Pink Panthers. If Mike had been in your front seat that day, in all probability—he would not have come home, either.

Odd, what brings people together. My friend, Mari Ann, swears you had a hand in this!

Who knows, maybe you did have something to do with it. I want you to know Mike is good to me and for me—so I know you would be pleased. We still have fun together and enjoy each other's company. We talk about going overseas someday—the wanderlust in him wants me to see more of the world like he has.

I'm glad Mike finally "talked to you" through a letter like I do. He told you why he gave up his seat that day. I doubt "what ifs" will ever go away, but over time one just has to learn to live with it. It's tough stuff because war is so ugly.

I can't say that this is my last letter. The last for right now, though. I'll "talk" to you the rest of my life. But I'm about to get real busy. I have a new project, Mark—I am going to write another book! Remember I told you about John Donovan, our cousin from Montgomery, Alabama, who was a Flying Tiger in 1942? He was a mercenary, a pilot, and a military man—I just know he would have been your hero. John wrote beautiful letters home while he was helping defend the Chinese people from the Japanese, and I have so many great pictures of him and the P-40s he flew.

The Flying Tigers, officially called the American Volunteer Group, disbanded in July of '42. John Wayne starred in a movie about the Flying Tigers that was a Hollywood hit. Americans loved it because they loved the Flying Tigers. Eventually, many of the Tigers wrote books about their experience. John was such an excellent writer, if he had survived, I think he might have written one, too. I want to tell John's story for him—I want to share John with others like I have shared you.

I look forward to the next chapter in my life. Look at all the wonderful people I've met since I began my journey to learn about you. It's going to be great and Mark—you will be the first to know!

Love always, Susie

EPILOGUE

...David Lee Collins
David Allen Curtis
Raymond Lee Dock, Jr.
Hallia Leon Griffin, Jr.
Joseph Guilmette Jr.
Joseph Justin Heltsley
Clark Holman
Thomas Edward Hughes
Michael Allen Mohowald
Tony Lee Martin
Daniel Dixon McNeill
Anthony Michael Notich
Phillip Allen Page
George J. Reed, Jr.
Larry A. Rush
Leroy H. Scott
Albert J. Smith
Harrel Earl Stearns
Rudolph Michael Stefanic
Sasa Uli
David E. Weiss
Marvin C. White
William G. White
Sammy H. Whitworth

I remember being told to watch for ice when I leave the podium, and turn toward the ramp. I place my feet flat and solid while I exit the stage and head down the ramp. More people have arrived and have taken their place in line. I see my dear friend Julie Kink near the end of the ramp. She's wearing her flight jacket with David's patches, and her black Cav hat. She arrived early to read her brother David's name. We both smile as I walk toward her and I know, almost like I read her mind—or maybe it's her heart that I know so well—she came early to hear me read Mark's name.

We hug, Linda joins us, and we talk quietly as we instinctively move towards our brothers' panels, away from the seating area. Linda takes our picture at panel 21, the panel between Mark's and David's panels. I subconsciously think it is wrong to smile. I always have. Like smiling at a funeral seems wrong. I know when I look at these pictures later, I'll be disappointed because I'll think I look awful—again.

I turn and rub my fingers over Mark's name, just as I've done a hundred times, and notice my reflection in the black granite. I look again, hoping to see Mark standing there, maybe with his hands on his hips—like pictures I have of him in Vietnam— black boots and green Army fatigues. His watch on the inside of his wrist. I look and imagine him there, because I want him to be there.

More people have arrived. It's getting crowded on The Wall walk-way. I notice people bending over to look at Mark's face and read the words to the song *Brother of Mine*. A teenage girl kneels, reads it and runs back a few panels to hasten her mother, so she can read it, too. I watch, but don't let on it was me who left it there. I hope they look at Mark's face. They both squat, then stand, find Mark's name on the panel and lightly run their fingertips over it. I smile. I smile, because I am so proud of him. I really do wish they knew he was my brother, but I am content to just watch. I've done this before. I wish I could leave his picture and the song every day, so more people will know how much I miss him—every day.

Those who have a loved one's name on The Wall know it really is every day. Those that have lost someone in Iraq or Afghanistan—they know, too. It's tough. But now, over forty years later, I know I am in the fifth and final stage of grief: Acceptance. Oh, acceptance doesn't mean it doesn't ever hurt or that I don't cry anymore. I'm done with the denial, the anger and the depression. I know Mark would want that and might even say to me, "What took so long!"

Julie's in line now to read. Linda and I have moved closer to hear her read David's name. Then it's time for us to drive back to Maryland, to spend time with Mother at Redina's. I'll see Julie again here tomorrow for the Veterans Day ceremony.

Like in Mike O'Donnell's poem, I instinctively look back at the Wall.

"...save one backward glance when you are leaving for the places they can no longer go.

...take one moment to embrace those gentle heroes you left behind."

Mark, you will always be my gentle hero.

ACKNOWLEDGEMENTS

JUST IN CASE THEY STILL don't know how much I appreciate each and every one of them: To all the men of the 361st AWC/ACE, The Pink Panthers, thank you from the bottom of my heart. You brought "leave no man behind" to a higher level.

Jedwin Smith, I know deep in my heart this book would not have come this far without you. Thank you for believing in me from the start. I appreciate every one of your red edit marks and I hope you stick with me through the next adventure. Thank you, brother!

To my writing group and writing class: we all know bringing this book to fruition "took a village." I appreciate each of you for your support and feedback. Mari Ann Stefanelli, your vision turned out to be my guiding light. You have been a true gift in my life—thank you! Carolyn Graham, I appreciate every moment of your love and constant support—thank you. See? God wasn't done with you yet, Sista!

To Mel Canon, and the entire Vietnam Helicopter Flight Crew Network group, thank you for your kindness and support since 1997.

Thank you to the board and members of The Combat Helicopter Pilots Association for your acceptance, support, and guidance. I appreciate being included as a legacy member.

Thank you to the members of The Vietnam Helicopter Pilots Association for welcoming Gold Star family members with open arms. You were the key to unlocking a past hidden away for far too many years.

Thank you, Gary Roush, for maintaining a database that provides vital information—right down to the tail numbers!

Thank you to my family for answering my many questions, listening to my endless babbling and for believing in me. Thank you for scanning old photos and sharing your memories of Mark. Family pictures and memories are scattered from coast-to-coast, but I think we regrouped them as best any family could.

A special thank you to John Plaster for writing the foreword and for always telling The Pink Panther story so well. You know—because you were there.

Thank you to my final editor, Ceilia Stratton.

A big hug and thank you to Julie Kink, Mike Sloniker, Jim Williams, Jack Taber, Bob Whitford, Art Cline, Ross Clement, Bill Reeder, Rick Huff, "Skip" Skipper, Jon Beckenhauer, Hank Cramer, Frank Thoman, Glynn Kohler, Mike Sheuerman and Kent Harper. All dear to me for different reasons, but the common denominator is Mark.

To all my children: I hope you are proud of this book and the history it provides future generations.

To my husband, Mike, thank you for believing in me. I appreciate your love and support more than you know.

RESOURCES

If you are in search of Military records or need replacement medals:
    National Personnel Records Center
    1 Archives Drive
    St. Louis, Missouri 63138

If you are in search of someone on The Wall virtually you can leave a thought, picture or memorial:
    www.virtualwall.org and www.vvmf.org

If you are a son or daughter of a KIA during the Vietnam War, Sons and Daughters in Touch is a wonderful support group:
    www.sdit.org

Statistics for the Vietnam War
    www.thewall-usa.com/names.asp

If you are in need of your DD 214(or if you are next of kin) Please don't wait until you *need* it, it's not quick.
    www.archives.gov/veterans/military-service-records/

GLOSSARY

A1E Skyraider Korean War era aircraft, single seat, able to carry a large assortment of bombs, fly at low altitude for long periods of time, and absorb heavy ground fire. Slang: Sandy

Agent Orange A herbicide containing trace amounts of the toxic contaminant dioxin that was used in the Vietnam War to defoliate areas of the forest.

AH-1G Also called the **Cobra** was the first helicopter to be originally designed as a gunship. Built by Bell Helicopter in Texas and introduced in Vietnam in 1967. Two seats: Pilot in the front seat and the Aircraft Commander in the slightly higher back seat. Slang: Snake

Air Medal The Air Medal is a United States military decoration awarded for meritorious achievement while participating in an aerial flight.

AO Area of Operation

Amateur Radio operated by trained, licensed individuals. Amateur Radio operators use their radio stations to make contact internationally or locally. Radios have been used on space stations by NASA astronauts like COL Doug Wheelock in recent years. (I wish Daddy had lived long enough to experience that.) Slang: Ham Radio

Army Commendation Medal The Army Commendation Medal is a mid-level United States military decoration which is awarded for sustained acts of heroism or meritorious service. For valorous actions in direct contact with the enemy, but of lesser degree than required for the award of the Bronze Star.

B-17 A Boeing heavy bomber airplane used during World War II. Capable of carrying over 17,000 pounds of ordinance. Speed 182 mph Slang: The Flying Fortress

B-24 A Boeing heavy bomber with a more modern design than the B-17. It was faster, carried heavier bombs and was more difficult to fly when compared to its predecessor. Called the Liberator but known to the crew as the Flying Coffin because of how difficult it was for the crew to escape if need be with a parachute on.

Battalion A battalion in the Army consists of 300-1000 soldiers, normally commanded by a Lieutenant Colonel. Within the battalion would be four to six companies.

C-141 Starlifter A Lockheed aircraft built under President Kennedy's first official act after his inauguration. The main purpose of the aircraft was to haul freight. Speed of 567 MPH and freight capacity of 202,000 pounds. Lockheed produced almost 300 during 1963-2006.

CAV Hat A black felt Stetson hat with a flexible brim worn by troopers of Cavalry units in the Army. Traditionally adorned with gold cord and cross sabers.

Cessna 150 A single engine, two seat airplane with tricycle gear. Used for student training, general aviation use. Maximum cruise speed of 124 mph.

Cessna 172 Skyhawk A single engine, four seat airplane, tricycle gear with maximum cruise speed of 142 mph

Cobra See AH-1G

Commanding Officer (CO) Pertaining to the 361ˢᵗ Aviation Co. Escort was always a Major. They were assigned to be in charge of the unit for no more than six months.

Camp Holloway Located Pleiku Province in the Central Highlands of South Vietnam II Corps.

Congressional Medal of Honor is the highest United States military award and the only medal with any monetary value to the recipient.

DD214 Military document includes condition of discharge, awards, education and length of service.

Distinguished Flying Cross (DFC) The cross symbolizes sacrifice, the colors are the colors of our nation, and the propeller symbolizes flight. It is awarded for heroism and achievement.

Dover is an Air Force Base in Dover, Delaware. It is also the largest military mortuary in the Department of Defense. Peacetime and wartime military dead are processed in Dover.

Everglades The largest subtropical wilderness in the United States located in South Florida.

Family Contacts Committee Volunteers work to connect a family member of a KIA to someone whom they served with in Vietnam. A labor of love. The committee was formed through the Vietnam Helicopter Flight Crew Network, an online list-server.

Flying Tigers The American Volunteer Group was formed by former military men, who resigned their commission, went to China to help the Chinese defend themselves against the Japanese in 1941. Disbanded July 14, 1942

Gladiators The 57ᵗʰ Assault Helicopter Company, an Army unit stationed in Kontum Province in Vietnam II Corps.

Gold Star A Gold Star pin is awarded to the Mother and Wife of military Killed-in-Action . Also eligible: the father, children and siblings.

Grumman OV-1 Mohawk A Turboprop armed military observation and attack aircraft. Crew of two, sitting side by side. Manufactured 1959-1970.

Gunship Sole purpose of a gunship is to provide protection with its weaponry.

Ho Chi Minh Trail A network of roads built between North Vietnam and South Vietnam through neighboring Laos and Cambodia. The trail is 2,500 miles long consisting of road, water and track. The name is American in origin. The Vietnamese name is Truong Son Road.

Huey UH-1 A utility helicopter made by Bell Helicopter with a crew of two officers and two enlisted. Most carried multiple weapons. Capable of carrying troops into the battle and injured and war dead out.

II Corps Pronounced *2 Core* was a portion of South Vietnam, divided for military purposes, that extended from the South China Sea to the Laotian and Cambodian borders in the Central Highlands.

Karmann Ghia A Volkswagen sports car imported in the United States until production ceased in 1974.

Kingsmen A unit of the 101st Aiborne Division

LOH or Light Observation Helicopter OH-06 made by Hughes a small helicopter capable of personnel transport, escort and attack missions, casualty evacuation and observation. Slang: Loach

LRRP Long Range Reconnaissance Patrol A small, heavily armed reconnaissance team that patrolled deep into enemy territory.

McGuire Rigs A rope type rig that was lowered below a hovering helicopter for emergency extraction of SOG recon soldiers.

Medal of Honor is the highest United States military award.

Medevac An unarmed helicopter for the rescue and transportation of injured military personnel to medical care.

Meritorious Showing merit. Deserving recognition and honor.

MIA Military term for Missing-in-Action

Montagnards South Vietnamese tribesmen, mercenaries, who worked side by side with our military in Vietnam . Slang: Yards

Naval Undersea Warfare Museum Keyport, Washington - One of twelve Naval Museums in the U.S.

Nomex Flame retardant material introduced by DuPont in the '60s and was the material used for flight suit or shirt and pants

Oak Leaf Cluster A bronze or silver oak leaf placed on the ribbon of a medal denotes the award has already been awarded. It represent subsequent awards.

Phoenix C/158 AHB 101 ABN (Airmobile) DIV

Pink Panthers 361ˢᵗ Aviation Company (Escort) Later 361ˢᵗ ACE stationed in Pleiku at Camp Holloway in the Central Highlands. II Corp

PTSD Post Traumatic Stress Disorder. A psychological condition originating from a traumatic event such a combat.

POW Prisoner of War

Purple Heart A military medal awarded for a combat injury or death.

Recon Team Reconnaissance team

RLO The Warrant Officers slang for Real Live Officer

Sharks 174th Attack Helicopter Company (also Dolphins) stationed in II Corps until 1967 then moved to Chu Lai, I Corp.

Special Forces Elite, highly trained personnel, performing unconventional covert guerilla warfare.

Vietnam Dustoff Association A nonprofit organization to promote camaraderie and the history of those who served in an aero-medical evacuation unit in Vietnam.

VHPA Vietnam Helicopter Pilots Association

Western Union Telegram best known for its war dead notification. A typed message carrying greetings of good or bad news began in 1851 and because of technology the only purpose of Western Union now is money wire transfers.

READERS GROUP GUIDE

DISCUSSION QUESTIONS

1. Did you learn anything about the Vietnam War that you didn't know before reading *Dear Mark*?

2. Was epistolary style easy for you to follow as a story? Would you read another book written this way?

3. Were you surprised at how the peace sign means different things to different people?

4. Do you think Susan might have been quicker to accept the fate of her brother had there been a viewing at the funeral? And burial in a cemetery?

5. If you were Susan would you have called Sherry twenty-seven years after losing Mark?

6. How would you have felt with the delivery of a telegram to inform you of the loss of a loved one?

7. Have you been to The Wall? Now that you have read *Dear Mark*, do the individual names on The Wall have more meaning to you?

8. Did you know you can find statistics online like how many father-sons, brothers, youngest and oldest died in Vietnam? http://www.thewall-usa.com/names.asp

9. Did you enjoy the book? Why? Or why not?

10. Have you ever wished you had told someone how proud you were of them or how much you loved them but they died—making it too late?

11. Are any of your family members veterans? Have you asked them about their military service?

12. If you are old enough, did this book take you back to the days of *peace, love, and rock and roll* of the '60s?

13. What was your favorite or most memorable passage in the book? Why did it make an impression?

14. Was the ending what you expected?

15. Would you recommend this book to others?